Language to go

PRE-INTERMEDIATE

STUDENTS' BOOK

Gillie Cunningham
Sue Mohamed

Series Editor: Simon Greenall

PEARSON
Longman

www.language-to-go.com

The past

Verb patterns

The present

Noun phrases

Modals

The future

Adjectives

Present perfect

Functions

Conditionals

Vocabulary   Regular and irregular verbs
Grammar   Past simple
Language to go   Talking about past events

A life of achievement

Speaking

1   **Speak to other students and find someone who:**

- is an only child
- isn't married
- has got a car
- hasn't got children
- lives in an apartment
- doesn't like chocolate
- can act
- can't play a musical instrument
- enjoyed reading as a child

Example:
A: *Are you an only child?*
B: *No, I've got two brothers.*

2   **Tell the class who you found for the things in Exercise 1.**

Example:
Julio is an only child.
Nobody can play a musical instrument.

Reading

3   **Read and answer about Oprah Winfrey. Which five things from the list in Exercise 1 are true for her?**

4   **Read again and complete Oprah Winfrey's lifeline with the correct years.**

Oprah Winfrey

People in more than 132 countries watch 'The Oprah Winfrey Show'. On this TV talk show, ordinary people talk about their problems and Oprah helps them. She lives in a wonderful apartment in Chicago, and has a farm and a house in the mountains. She has great cars and a plane too. But Oprah Winfrey was not always rich and famous.

What sort of life did Oprah have as a child?

Oprah Winfrey was born in 1954 in Mississippi, USA.

Her family didn't have a lot of money. Oprah could read and write when she was three and she loved books. She worked hard and was an excellent student at school, but she left college when she was nineteen and didn't finish her education.

How did she start her successful career?

She wanted to be famous and found a job in TV. She was the first woman and the first black person to read the TV news in Nashville. In 1977, she had her first TV talk show. In 1984, she

1 Oprah Winfrey was born.

3 She had her first talk show.

1954

2 She left college and found her first job in TV.

4 She started 'The Oprah Winfrey Show'.

moved to Chicago and started 'The Oprah Winfrey Show'. It was a great success.

What did she do later?

In 1985, Oprah acted in Steven Spielberg's movie *The Color Purple*. She didn't have any children, but she used her success to help other people's children. She gave hundreds of thousands of dollars to students so they could go to college and in 1997 she started the charity Angel Network to build houses for people in need.

Oprah in *The Color Purple*

5 She acted in her first movie.

6 She started a charity to help other people.

Grammar focus

5 **Look at the examples below. Is this explanation true (T) or false (F)?**

We use the past simple to talk about completed actions in the past.

Past simple	
Regular	**Irregular**
e.g. *love, work, finish, end, want, move, act, use*	e.g. *be, can, leave, find, do, give*
(?) How *did* she *start* her successful career?	What sort of life *did* she *have* as a child?
(+) She *started* 'The Oprah Winfrey Show' in 1984.	She *had* her first talk show in 1977.
(–) She *didn't start* Angel Network in 1984.	Her family *didn't have* a lot of money.

6 📼 **Listen and repeat the regular past simple forms. How do you pronounce verbs that end in -ted or -ded?**

Practice

7 **Rewrite this text in the past simple. Begin like this:**

Yesterday, Karl Jones worked very hard.

Karl Jones works very hard. He starts his day early, at 5.30 a.m. He has a meeting with his directors at 10 a.m. They give him ideas for new projects. He doesn't want to work late but he doesn't leave until 9 p.m. And what does he do at home? More work, of course!

Get talking

8 **Talk about your lifeline.**

1 Draw your lifeline. Include dates but no other information.

2 In pairs, ask and answer questions to guess the missing information in your lifelines.

Example:
A: *Did you get married in 2001?*
B: *No, I bought my first car.*

3 Tell the class something interesting about your partner.

Example: *She bought her first car in 2001.*

Language to go

A: When did you leave school?
B: In 1999. I didn't want to go to university so I found a job.

> GRAMMAR REFERENCE PAGE 110

> PRACTICE PAGE 90

1

Vocabulary   Free time activities
Grammar   Likes / dislikes + *-ing* form + qualifying adverbs
Language to go   Saying how much you like doing things

Billy Elliot

Vocabulary and speaking

1   **Put the free time activities in the correct columns.**

> box   football   golf   gymnastics
> volleyball   run   yoga   swim   ballet

verb only	*play +* ...	*do +* ...
box	football	

2   **In pairs, discuss these questions.**

1   Who in your family does the activities above?

   Example: *Nobody swims.*
   My grandfather plays football.

2   Which of the activities are more often done:
   a) by men?   b) by women?

Reading

3   **Read the film review and answer the questions.**

1   Which activities in Exercise 1 does Billy do?
2   Which activity does his family dislike?

4   **Read again and complete the sentences.**

1   Billy's father likes _drinking_ and _____ .
2   His brother likes _____ , _____ and
   _____ .
3   Billy likes _____ , _____
   and _____ .
4   He doesn't like _____ or
   _____ .

film REVIEW

BILLY ELLIOT is a film about a boy from the north of England and his love for ballet. Billy's mother is dead. His brother and father are miners during the 1980s miners' strike. Life is difficult and their only relaxation is at the miners' social club, where they enjoy drinking and arguing.

Billy's brother also likes listening to rock music and Billy does too. At school, Billy quite likes playing football but he doesn't like running or other sports very much. His father wants him to box and gives him money for lessons at the social club. After a few lessons, Billy decides that he hates boxing. There's a ballet

Grammar focus

5 **Look at the examples below and underline the correct words in these explanations.**

1 Verbs for likes and dislikes can be followed by an *infinitive / -ing form*.
2 We use *really / quite* to express our likes and dislikes more strongly.

Expressing likes and dislikes

(+) Billy *loves dancing*.
(−) He *doesn't like running*.
(?) What *do* you *like doing*?

Qualifying adverbs

(++) I *really* love it.
(+) I *quite* enjoy it.
(−) I *don't* like it *very much*.
(− −) I *really* hate it.

---

6 📖 **Listen and repeat the examples above. Pay attention to intonation.**

class at the same time and Billy prefers watching that. The ballet teacher asks him to join the class and Billy finds he really loves dancing.

Billy's father and brother are furious and tell him to stop. But Billy continues doing ballet in secret. Finally his father understands: dancing can help Billy have a better life. He takes Billy to London and Billy gets a place at the Royal School of Ballet.

This film is based on the true-life story of Philip Mosley. The acting is superb and you will laugh and cry from beginning to end. ∎

Practice

7 **Write sentences using the verbs and adverbs suggested in brackets.**

Example: Gerry / listen / music (+ like)
Gerry quite likes listening to music.

1 Felipe / go / football matches (++ love)
2 Sarah / play / volleyball (− − hate)
3 Trevor and Simon / watch / TV (− enjoy)
4 Oscar / box (+ enjoy)
5 Paula / do / ballet (− like)
6 I / do / yoga (+ like)
7 We / play / golf (++ enjoy)

Get talking …

8 **Talk about your free time activities.**

1 Individually, complete your part of the table. Put ++, +, − or − − to show how much you like or dislike doing each activity.

2 In pairs, ask and answer questions to complete the table for your partner.
Example:
A: **Do you like dancing?**
B: **Yes, I really love it. (++) / No, I don't like it very much. (−)**

3 Report your partner's answers to the class.

4 Find out which activities are more popular with men in the class, and which are more popular with women.

Free time activities

	You	Your partner
dancing	○	○
listening to classical music	○	○
watching boxing matches	○	○
going to the ballet	○	○
going to the theatre	○	○
playing football	○	○
doing other sports	○	○

… and writing

9 **Write a report of your results.**

Example: **I quite like dancing but my partner really hates it. We both quite enjoy listening to …**

Language to go

A: Do you enjoy doing sport?
B: Well, I really love watching it but I don't like doing it very much.

> GRAMMAR REFERENCE PAGE 110
> PRACTICE PAGE 90

LESSON 3
The present

Vocabulary   Clothes; weather and seasons
Grammar   Present simple and present continuous
Language to go   Comparing usual and present situations

Hurricane

spring

summer

autumn

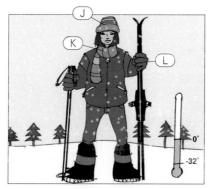

winter

Vocabulary and speaking

1   Choose three sentences for each picture.

Example: It's raining. – *autumn*

1 It's 35°C.   5 It's really cold.   9 It's raining.
2 It's –32°C.   6 It's really hot.   10 It's snowing.
3 It's 18°C.   7 It's quite warm.   11 It's sunny.
4 It's 12°C.   8 It's quite cool.   12 It's windy.

2   Match the words with the clothes in the pictures.

Example: umbrella – *G*

> hat   gloves   umbrella   boots   shorts   T-shirt
> jacket   sunhat   scarf   coat   sandals   sweater

3   Answer these questions about the weather where you live.

1 Do you have spring, summer, autumn and winter?
2 What is the average temperature in these months?
   a) December   b) April   c) August
3 What is your favourite time of year? Why?

Listening

4   In pairs, decide which three of these places often have hurricanes.

> Chicago   the Dominican Republic
> Montreal   Miami   Seattle   Puerto Rico

5   Listen and answer true (T) or false (F).

Example: The hurricane's name is Charlie. *T*

1 The hurricane is in Puerto Rico.
2 They know this hurricane is a big one.
3 The hurricane is there now.
4 Most of the people are staying.
5 Some people are trying to protect their homes.
6 People are carrying umbrellas.
7 These weather conditions happen quite often.
8 People live there because it's beautiful.

Grammar focus

6 **Look at the examples below and complete these explanations with the *present simple* or *present continuous*.**

1 We use the _____ to talk about time around the present moment.
2 We use the _____ to talk about what usually happens.
3 We generally use the _____ with verbs like *know*, *think* and *understand*.

Present simple	Present continuous
We *know* it's a big one. Some people *stay*.	Lots of people *are leaving* Miami.

Practice

7 **Complete the sentences with the correct form of the present simple or present continuous.**

1 I <u>know</u> (know) the UK _____ (not usually have) very cold weather, but it's very cold at the moment. It _____ (snow) and the temperature is –8°C. People _____ (stay) at home.

2 It's usually cold in February and it _____ (rain) a lot, but today the sun _____ (shine) and it's a very warm 22°C. People _____ (wear) their summer clothes and they _____ (not carry) umbrellas as they usually _____ (do).

3 I _____ (think) spring in the UK is very beautiful. People usually _____ (wear) sweaters and jackets.

4 It often _____ (rain) in summer in the UK and sometimes it's quite cold. But occasionally we _____ (have) very hot weather with temperatures above 30°C. Today isn't one of those days. It _____ (rain) and everyone _____ (wear) raincoats.

5 In the autumn it _____ (get) dark at about 6 p.m. but in summer it _____ (not get) dark until 10 p.m.

Get writing ...

8 **An American friend is coming to your country for a year. Write an e-mail answering his / her questions.**

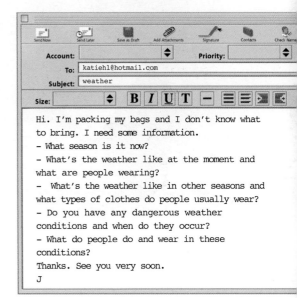

Hi. I'm packing my bags and I don't know what to bring. I need some information.
– What season is it now?
– What's the weather like at the moment and what are people wearing?
– What's the weather like in other seasons and what types of clothes do people usually wear?
– Do you have any dangerous weather conditions and when do they occur?
– What do people do and wear in these conditions?
Thanks. See you very soon.
J

... and talking

9 **In pairs, compare your e-mails. Are you both sending similar information?**

Language to go

A: What's the weather like?
B: The sun's shining. It doesn't always rain in London.

> GRAMMAR REFERENCE PAGE 110
> PRACTICE PAGE 91

Vocabulary   Possessions
Grammar   Possessive *'s*, possessive adjectives / pronouns, *belong to*
Language to go   Talking about what belongs to us

Possessions we hate

watch

mini-disk player

ROOM 101

radio

camera

mobile phone

guitar

Vocabulary and speaking

1   Put the possessions in the picture in order of importance (1–8)
for you. In pairs, compare your answers.

2   [cassette] Listen and put words you hear in the correct sound
group. How is the letter *a* pronounced each time?

man	what	car	sofa	day
camera				

3   In groups, discuss the possessions which irritate you most.

Example: My camera, because I can never put the film in
properly and it takes bad pictures.

Reading and listening

4   **Read about the TV
programme 'Room 101',
opposite, and answer the
questions.**

1 What is Room 101 in
George Orwell's book?
2 What do guests on the TV
programme do?

Grammar focus

7 Look at the examples below. Which question do they answer?

a) What is it?   b) Whose is it?

Possessive 's	Possessive adjective	Possessive pronoun	*belong to* + object pronoun
It's *Paul's* guitar.	It's *his* guitar.	It's *his*.	It *belongs to him*.
It's *Andrea's* phone.	It's *her* phone.	It's *hers*.	It *belongs to her*.
It's *my parents'* TV.	It's *their* TV.	It's *theirs*.	It *belongs to them*.

Practice

8 Rewrite these sentences using the correct form of the words in brackets.

Example: The guitar is yours, Paul. (your)
It's your guitar, Paul.

1 The mini-disk player is Anna's. (belong)
2 The video camera belongs to David. ('s)
3 The TV belongs to us. (ours)
4 The mobile phone belongs to John. ('s)
5 The radio is Meg and Jo's. (theirs)
6 It's Caroline's watch. (her)
7 Katy has got a camera. ('s)
8 It's Daniel's laptop. (belong)

Get talking

9 Take part in the TV programme 'Room 101'.

1 Individually, choose three possessions to put in Room 101.
  • Choose one of your own possessions and two that belong to friends or other people in your family.
  • Think about why you want to put them in the room.

2 In pairs, talk about the things you chose.
  • Say why you want to put each thing in Room 101.
  • Say what your partner can / can't put in Room 101 and why.

TV

laptop

ROOM 101

TONIGHT the TV show 'Room 101' returns to BBC2. The idea for this popular TV programme comes from the science fiction book *1984* by George Orwell. In the book, Room 101 contains the thing that frightens each person the most. In the programme, guests talk about things they hate and want to throw into Room 101.

5 ▭ Listen to the programme and answer the questions.

1 What possessions does Andrea want to put in Room 101?
2 Which possessions can she put there?
3 Who decides?

6 Listen again. Whose is each possession?

Language to go

A: It doesn't belong to you.
   It belongs to both of us.
B: Listen, what's yours is mine but what's mine is my own!

> GRAMMAR REFERENCE PAGE 110
> PRACTICE PAGE 91

LESSON 5
Modals

Vocabulary   Weddings
Grammar   *Should / shouldn't* and imperatives
Language to go   Giving advice

A Scottish wedding

Vocabulary

1 Replace the words in
brackets with words from
the box.

> guests reception
> groom honeymoon
> bride   best man
> bridesmaids

A Traditional Scottish Wedding

The <u>groom</u> (man who gets married) arrives after the guests but before the (1)_____ (woman who gets married). She sometimes arrives late. She usually has three or four (2)_____ (women / girls who help her). They walk behind her into the church. After the wedding ceremony, the (3)_____ (friends and family at the wedding) are usually invited to a (4)_____ (wedding party) where everyone eats, drinks and dances. The (5)_____ (man who helps the groom) reads cards and makes a speech. The married couple dance all night and then go on their (6)_____ (holiday).

Listening

2  **Listen to 'Get it right!', Dee Carson's cultural advice show on American radio.**

1 Where is the listener, Chad Barnes, going?
2 What does he want to know?

3 **Listen again. Is this advice true (T) or false (F)?**

Example: Don't go to the wedding. **F**

1 Don't wear a kilt.
2 Don't check the wedding list before you buy a present.
3 Don't give money.
4 Don't sit on the left if you are a friend of the groom.
5 Don't dance first at the reception.

Grammar focus

4 **Look at the examples below and complete these sentences with *is* or *isn't*.**

1 It _____ a good idea to check the wedding list.
2 It _____ a good idea to give money.

Asking for and giving advice	
should + infinitive (without *to*)	Imperatives
(?) What present *should* I *take*?	
(+) You *should check* the wedding list.	*Enjoy* yourself.
(–) You *shouldn't give* money.	*Don't dance* first.

Practice

5 **Complete the sentences with the correct form of *should* and the verbs in brackets.**

1 A: What <u>should</u> a British groom <u>do</u> (do) on his wedding morning?
   B: I'm not sure. But he definitely _____ (not see) the bride.
2 A: Traditionally, how _____ a French couple _____ (go) from the town hall to the church?
   B: They _____ (walk).
3 A: In the USA, _____ you _____ (give) just one wedding present or more?
   B: They have lots of pre-wedding parties or 'showers'. You _____ (give) a present at each 'shower'.
4 A: In the USA you _____ (not dance) first.
   B: Why _____ you _____ (do) that?
   A: Because the newly married couple _____ (dance) first.

6 **In pairs, practise the dialogues.**

Get talking ...

7 **In groups, give advice to a Scottish friend coming to a wedding in your country.**

1 Discuss differences and similarities between a Scottish wedding and a traditional wedding in your country.

Think about:
• entertainment
• other traditions
• clothes
• presents
• food
• drink

2 Choose five main pieces of advice to give your friend.

... and writing

8 **Write giving advice to your Scottish friend. Start like this:**

Dear ... ,

Here are some things you should know before you come to the wedding. First, you should ...

Language to go

A: What should she wear to the wedding?
B: She should wear a dress.
   She shouldn't wear trousers.

> GRAMMAR REFERENCE PAGE 111
> PRACTICE PAGE 92

Vocabulary   Countries and continents
Grammar   The future with *going to*
Language to go   Talking about future plans

Travel with English

Vocabulary and speaking

1   **Match these continents with the countries in the travel article.**

Example: *Africa – South Africa*

| Africa   Europe   Asia   Australasia   America |

2   🔊 **Listen and repeat. Put each country in the correct stress group.**

☐ ▫	☐ ▫ ▫	▫ ☐ ▫ ▫
Po land	It a ly	Co lom bi a

3   **In pairs, discuss which countries you want to visit and why.**

I want to visit ...

Reading

4   **Read the article and complete the table.**

	When to visit	What to see / do
Australia		Sydney outdoor life water sports
South Africa		
India		
Canada	November	
Ireland		

THE TRAVEL WRITER'S

Dream holiday

*I've got five months to travel before I write!
I'm going to explore countries where I can
speak English. Where am I going to start?*

AUSTRALIA

Australia is particularly hot from November to
March. I love hot weather so I'm going to
arrive in Sydney in December. There's a lot of
outdoor life, and water sports to keep you cool.

SOUTH AFRICA

South Africa offers luxury safaris and the
chance to see lots of exotic animals. It also has
a wonderful coastline so, after the safari, I'm
going to find a beach and swim. I like the sun
so I'm going to go in February.

Grammar focus

5 Look at the examples below. Is this explanation true (T) or false (F)?

We use *be + going to +* infinitive to talk about future plans.

The future with *going to*

(+) I *'m going to spend* a month in India.
(–) She *isn't going to visit* the Inuits in Canada.
(?) *Are* you *going to arrive* in December?
(Yes, I *am.* / No, I *'m not.*)

INDIA

Rajasthan is the perfect 'India for beginners' with its colours, views and monuments. There are also exciting markets to visit, with beautiful clothes and jewellery. I'm going to spend a month there in January. That's when they say the weather is really good.

CANADA

It's the Rockies for me in November! There are mountains and beautiful lakes everywhere. I'd like to visit the Inuits in the north of Canada too, but unfortunately I'm not going to get there ... there isn't enough time.

IRELAND

In March I'm going to take part in the St Patrick's Day festivities but I know it can be cold. I'm going to buy a beautiful Irish sweater to take back home. Dublin is a great city and there's fantastic countryside too, so Ireland should be fun.

Practice

6 Complete the sentences with the correct form of *be going to* and the verbs in brackets.

Example: When <u>is he going to leave</u> (he leave) Dublin?

1 Laura _____ (see) beautiful monuments in India.
2 We _____ (walk) by the lakes in Canada.
3 _____ (we swim) in the sea in South Africa?
4 I _____ (visit) Alice Springs and other famous places in Australia.
5 Alex _____ (take part) in the St Patrick's Day festivities in Ireland.
6 They _____ (not stay) in luxury accommodation in South Africa.
7 _____ (you climb) any mountains in Canada?
8 She _____ (not travel) to Australia in July when the weather is cold.

Get talking

7 Plan a group holiday to three countries where you can use your English.

1 Individually, look at the article again:
  • Which three countries / continents do you most want to visit? Why?
  • In which three months do you want to go?

2 In groups, tell other students your choice.
  I want to go to ... in ... because ...

3 Vote to decide where and when your group is going to go. Discuss what you are going to do when you get there.

4 Tell the class your group's decisions. Can you make it a class holiday?

> GRAMMAR REFERENCE PAGE 111
> PRACTICE PAGE 92

Language to go

A: **What** are you going to do next summer?
B: I'm going to fly around the world.

Vocabulary   Adjectives to describe character
Grammar   Comparatives
Language to go   Making comparisons

Why women iron

Vocabulary and speaking

1 <u>Underline</u> the correct adjectives.

Example: Mike's very *talkative* / <u>*hardworking*</u>. He studies every night.

1 My brother is a very *messy* / *tidy* person. He never cleans his room.
2 You need two hours to phone Linda. She's very *talkative* / *messy*.
3 Helen is very *cooperative* / *competitive*. It's great to work with her.
4 Your house always looks nice. You're very *aggressive* / *tidy*.
5 I'm good at tennis but I don't often win. I'm not very *cooperative* / *competitive*.
6 Jack's very *aggressive* / *cooperative*. Nobody wants to work with him.

2 **In pairs, describe the character and behaviour of the people in the photos. Use adjectives from Exercise 1.**

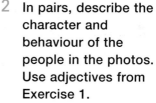

Reading

3 **Discuss which adjectives from Exercise 1 usually describe:**

a) men   b) women

4 **Read the text. Do the authors agree with you?**

5 **Read the text again. In pairs, answer the questions.**

1 What do many people believe about men's behaviour?
2 What do these people think modern men should do?
3 Do the Moirs think men can change very much?
4 What do you think? Are men and women born with different behaviour or do they learn it?

Why Men Don't Iron

by Anne and Bill Moir
HARPERCOLLINS ISBN 0-006-531008

BOOK OF THE WEEK A lot of people believe that society – our family, friends and teachers – teaches boys and girls to behave differently. They say that as adults we should change this. The 'new man' should cook, look after the children, be more emotional and less aggressive. He should be tidier, more cooperative and a better listener. But is this change impossible for men? Can men be as cooperative as women, for example?

The differences are obvious from a very early age. At school, boys are messier and more competitive than girls: boys like to win! But girls are better students: they're more hardworking than boys and they do more homework. Girls may be more talkative than boys, but boys are noisier. Some doctors believe that baby girls are stronger than baby boys. But at school age, girls aren't as strong as boys. Why? Does society change us?

In their book *Why Men Don't Iron* Anne and Bill Moir explain their view that men are more aggressive, more active, etc., because they are **born** that way. And society can't change their behaviour.

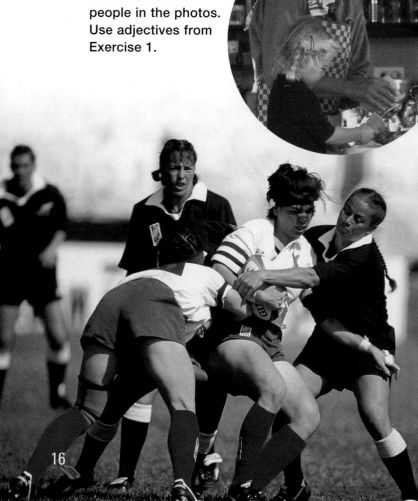

Grammar focus

6 Look at the examples below and match the two halves of these explanations.

1 To make comparative sentences with 1-syllable adjectives (e.g. *strong*),
2 To make comparative sentences with 2-syllable adjectives ending in *y* (e.g. *messy*),
3 To make comparative sentences with 2 / 3 / 4-syllable adjectives (e.g. *competitive*),
4 In sentences with *(not) as ... as*,

a) add *more ... (than)*.
b) use the adjective, not the comparative form.
c) change *y* to *i* and add *-er (than)*.
d) add *-er (than)*.

Comparative adjectives	*(not) as* + adjective + *as*
Boys are *stronger than* girls.	= Girls aren't *as strong as* boys.
Boys are *messier than* girls.	= Girls aren't *as messy as* boys.
Boys are *more competitive than* girls.	= Girls aren't *as competitive as* boys.
Girls are *better** students *than* boys.	= Boys aren't *as good* students *as* girls.

*Irregular comparatives: good – *better than* bad – *worse than*

Practice

7 Rewrite the sentences so that they have the same meaning.

Example: Women aren't as strong as men.
Men are <u>stronger than women</u>.

1 Boys are faster than girls.
  Girls aren't as _____ .
2 Girls aren't as noisy as boys.
  Boys are _____ .
3 Men aren't as talkative as women.
  Women are _____ .
4 Women are tidier than men.
  Men aren't as _____ .
5 Women aren't as messy as men.
  Men are _____ .
6 Schoolgirls are more hardworking than schoolboys.
  Schoolboys aren't as _____ .
7 Boys are better than girls at football.
  Girls aren't as _____ .

8 🎧 Listen and check your answers.

9 Listen again and practise the sentences. Pay attention to linking.

Example: Girls aren't as fast as boys.

Get talking

10 Compare male and female behaviour.

1 Complete the questionnaire below. What do you think?

2 In groups, compare your opinions and discuss any differences.

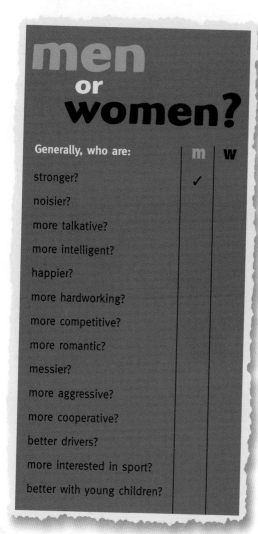

men or women?

Generally, who are:	m	w
stronger?	✓	
noisier?		
more talkative?		
more intelligent?		
happier?		
more hardworking?		
more competitive?		
more romantic?		
messier?		
more aggressive?		
more cooperative?		
better drivers?		
more interested in sport?		
better with young children?		

Language to go

A: He's stronger and more competitive than me.
B: But is he as fast as you?

> GRAMMAR REFERENCE PAGE 111
> PRACTICE PAGE 93

Vocabulary   Adventure sports
Grammar   Present perfect and past simple
Language to go   Talking about past experiences

E

Take a risk

B

C

A

ADVENTURE ZONE HOLIDAYS

D

Vocabulary

1   Match the words with the photos.

Example: waterskiing – C

1 rock climbing
2 scuba diving
3 windsurfing
4 snowboarding
5 skateboarding

2   Listen and repeat. Put each word in the correct stress group.

☐	☐	☐	☐	☐	☐	☐
wa	ter	ski	ing			

Listening

3   Listen and answer true (T) or false (F).

1 Andy is on holiday.   2 Paula is on holiday.

4   Listen again and put ticks (✓) and crosses (✗) in the table.

	waterskiing		windsurfing		scuba diving		rock climbing	
	yes	enjoyed	yes	enjoyed	yes	enjoyed	yes	enjoyed
Andy	✓	✓						
Paula								

5   Listen to Andy again and underline the correct verb forms.

DAVE: Right, Andy. *Did you do* / *Have you done* any dangerous sports before?

ANDY: Yes, *I played* / *I've played* football – that's pretty dangerous. And *I went* / *I've been* waterskiing and rock climbing, but only once.

DAVE: Waterskiing and rock climbing? When *did you do* / *have you done* that, then?

ANDY: On my vacation in Greece, last year.

DAVE: And what *did you think* / *have you thought* of them?

ANDY: Well, *I really enjoyed* / *I've really enjoyed* waterskiing ...

Grammar focus

6 **Look at the examples below and complete these explanations with the *present perfect* or *past simple*.**

1 We form the _____ with *have* or *has* and the past participle.
2 We use the _____ to talk about finished actions in the past.
3 We use the _____ to talk about our experiences. We don't need to say when the experiences happened.

Present perfect	Past simple
(?) *Have* you ever *done* any dangerous sports? (Yes, I *have*. / No, I *haven't*.)	When *did* you *do* that?
(+) I*'ve played* football.	I *played* football last Saturday.
(–) I *haven't been* windsurfing.	I *didn't go* windsurfing yesterday.

	Infinitive	Past simple	Past participle
Regular:	play	played	played
Irregular:	do	did	done
	go	went	gone / been*

* *gone* = go somewhere   * *been* = go somewhere and come back

Practice

7 **Complete the sentences with the correct form of the present perfect or past simple.**

1 A: **Have you ever played** (you ever play) football?
   B: No, I _____ .

2 A: _____ (you watch) that programme about rock climbing last night?
   B: Yes, I _____ . It _____ (be) really interesting.

3 A: _____ (your sister ever run) in a marathon?
   B: No, she _____ , but she _____ (run) in a half marathon last week.

4 A: _____ (you enjoy) that adventure holiday last summer?
   B: No, I _____ . It _____ (be) really terrible.

5 A: I _____ (never do) any dangerous sports. Have you?
   B: Yes, I _____ (go) scuba diving for the first time last month.
   A: _____ (you like) it?
   B: Yes, I _____ (have) a wonderful time.

8 **In pairs, practise the dialogues.**

Get talking ...

9 **Ask and answer about your sporting experiences.**

1 Choose four dangerous sports and make questions.
   Have you ever ... ?

2 Talk to other students and find out:
   • who has done these sports
   • who enjoyed / hated them
   • who wants to try them
   • who has only watched them
   • what other sports they've done (were they dangerous?)

... and writing

10 **Write a paragraph to complete your application form for an Adventure Zone holiday.**

Example:
I've been waterskiing and ...

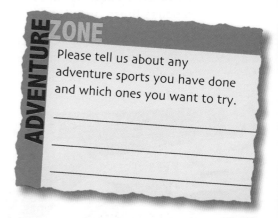

ADVENTURE ZONE

Please tell us about any adventure sports you have done and which ones you want to try.

_____
_____
_____

Language to go

A: Have you ever done any dangerous sports?
B: Yes, I played football last week and broke my leg.

> GRAMMAR REFERENCE PAGE 111
> PRACTICE PAGE 93

Vocabulary   At the office: verb + noun combinations
Function   Offers and requests
Language to go   Making and responding to offers and requests

Job share

Vocabulary

1 **Complete the sentences with the correct form of the verbs in the box.**

| leave   get   send   sign   have   arrange   do (x2)   make (x2) |

Example: Where's your report? I <u>**sent**</u> you a fax about it yesterday.

1 I haven't read your fax. I only _____ it a minute ago.
2 Can I _____ a message for Miss Parker, please?
3 We need to _____ a meeting for next Friday.
4 Can you _____ the filing, please? There's paper all over the office.
5 Please don't _____ personal phone calls at work.
6 We _____ a very useful meeting yesterday. We _____ some important decisions.
7 I can't _____ the photocopying now. I'm too busy.
8 Can you _____ your name here, please?

Reading and speaking

2 **Read the newspaper article and look at the photos. In pairs, discuss these questions.**

1 Which of these jobs can / can't people share easily?
2 What problems can there be when people share a job?

Listening

3 🔲 **Ken and Pat share a job at a model agency. Listen and answer the questions.**

1 What job do they share?
2 What is the problem?

4 **Listen again and answer true (T) or false (F).**

Example:
Ken is happy to do Pat's jobs. **F**

1 Pat answered the phone a lot yesterday.
2 Pat sent the faxes yesterday.
3 Ken isn't going to send the faxes.
4 Pat didn't phone the photographer yesterday.
5 Mr Davis asked Ken to book the restaurant.
6 Pat is going to arrange everything for the meeting.

a taxi driver

a musician

Could you share your job?

THERE ARE 1.3 million people without jobs in this country. People with jobs often say that they have too much work and no time to relax with the family. Is the answer job sharing? Of course, the idea of another person doing half your job is wonderful, but what about getting half your usual pay?

Language focus

5 **Look at the examples below and answer these questions.**

1 Which examples are requests (asking people to do things for you)?
2 Which examples are offers (saying you will do things for other people)?

Offers and requests

1 A: *Can you phone* the restaurant, please?
 B: Yes, of course.
2 A: *Could you do* this photocopying?
 B: Sorry, I'm afraid I can't.
3 A: *I'll (I will) send* the faxes today.
 B: Thank you.
4 A: *Shall I arrange* a meeting for you?
 B: Yes, please.

---

6 🔲 **Listen and practise the dialogues above. Pay attention to intonation.**

a secretary

a teacher

Practice

7 **Complete the dialogues with *shall / will / can* or *could*. Use the words in brackets.**

1 A: <u>Shall I phone</u> (I phone) the station for you?
 B: Yes, please. _____ (you book) me a ticket on the 10 a.m. train?
2 A: _____ (you write) the report?
 B: OK. Then _____ (I give) it to James for you.
3 A: _____ (I arrange) the meeting for you. Is Friday OK?
 B: Yes, fine. And _____ (you send) an e-mail to Bernie about it?
4 A: _____ (I order) you a taxi?
 B: No. Don't worry. I can do that. But _____ (you check) the flight time for me, please?

8 **In pairs, practise the dialogues.**

Get talking

9 **Roleplay a dialogue between a boss and his / her secretary.**

1 In pairs, rewrite the dialogue below. Use requests and offers to make it more polite.

   Example: *Could you send this fax ... ?*

2 Practise the dialogue with your partner.

A: Send this fax to Peter Fox.
B: The fax machine is broken.
A: Send an e-mail to Fox.
B: Give me Fox's e-mail address.
A: Here you are.
B: What shall I write?
A: Ask Fox to come to the Friday meeting. Book a restaurant for Friday evening for ten people.
B: OK, a table at the Lemon Tree restaurant.
A: That's fine.

Language to go

A: Could you lend me some money, please?
B: Again! Don't worry, I'll pay for you.

> GRAMMAR REFERENCE PAGE 111
> PRACTICE PAGE 94

Vocabulary   Verbs and their opposites
Grammar   Zero conditional (*if* + present form + present form)
Language to go   Talking about consequences

Behave yourself

Vocabulary

1 Match each verb with its opposite.

Example: **1 – b)**

1 open	a) empty
2 give	b) close
3 come	c) borrow
4 fill	d) forget
5 lend	e) go
6 push	f) take
7 remember	g) pull

2 Underline the correct words in these sentences.

Example: In some countries, you can't buy anything in the middle of the day because the shops *open* / *close* for lunch.

1 Don't forget to *give* / *borrow* me your key so I can get in.
2 Can you *take* / *lend* me your pen, please?
3 He *pushed* / *filled* the car with petrol before he went home.
4 I was really pleased when they *remembered* / *came* my birthday.
5 She needs some money so she shouldn't *forget* / *lend* to go to the bank.
6 I entered the room and *pulled* / *emptied* the door closed behind me.

How do **you** behave?

❶

If you forget a friend's birthday, do you:
a) send a card immediately and say the post is slow?
b) send a card now and say sorry?
c) send no card and say it's lost in the post?

❷

If someone pushes his / her trolley in front of you in a supermarket, do you:
a) look angry but say nothing?
b) ask the person politely to stop?
c) push his / her trolley back?

❸

If a friend gives you a present you really don't like, do you:
a) take it but never use it?
b) take it and only use it when your friend is there?
c) take it and give it to someone else?

KEY
Mainly a) answers: You behave quite well but you aren't always honest.
Mainly b) answers: You behave very well.
Mainly c) answers: You don't behave very well at all. Try harder!

Reading and speaking

3 **Do the questionnaire below. Then check the key.**

4 **In pairs, compare your behaviour.**

1 Read the questionnaire again and guess your partner's answers.

2 Take turns to ask and answer the questions. How many of your partner's answers did you guess correctly?

3 Who behaves better? Who is more honest?

4

If someone borrows money from you and forgets to pay you back, do you:
a) say you need some money and hope the person remembers?
b) ask him / her for the money?
c) refuse to lend him / her money again?

5

A friend cancels a night out with you saying he / she has to work. If you see him / her later that evening at the cinema, do you:
a) say nothing?
b) say what you think?
c) refuse to go out with him / her again?

Grammar focus

5 **Look at the examples below and underline the correct words in the explanation.**

The result *depends / doesn't depend* on the *if* clause.

Zero conditional	
If clause	Result
(+) *If* I *forget* a friend's birthday,	I *send* a card later.
(−) *If* I *don't remember* a friend's birthday,	I *don't send* a card.
(?) *If* you *forget* a friend's birthday,	*do* you *say* sorry?

Practice

6 **Complete the zero conditional sentences with the correct form of the verbs in brackets.**

Example: If he *doesn't like* (not like) the food in a restaurant, he *sends* (send) it back.

1 If the car _____ (not start) in the morning, we push it.
2 If the weather _____ (be) bad, _____ (you drive) the children to school?
3 If my daughter _____ (get) angry with her brother, she _____ (pull) his hair.
4 If he _____ (not come) home at ten o'clock, his mother _____ (phone) his friends.
5 If I _____ (not have) enough money, I _____ (borrow) it.
6 If his friends _____ (ask) him, _____ (he lend) them his car?

Get talking and writing

7 **Ask and answer more questions about behaviour.**

1 In pairs, think of three more questions for the questionnaire. Think about behaviour in shops, restaurants or family situations.

2 Write down your questions. Begin each one with *If ... ?* and give three possible types of behaviour, labelled a), b) and c).

3 Answer another pair's questions.

Language to go

A: What do you do if you need money?
B: If it's for something important, I work extra hours.

> GRAMMAR REFERENCE PAGE 112
> PRACTICE PAGE 94

LESSON **11**
The past

Vocabulary Customs: verb + noun combinations
Grammar *Used to / didn't use to*
Language to go Talking about past customs

Customs change

Vocabulary and speaking

1 Complete the questions with verbs from the box.

> have stay open play wear (x2)
> lock take off put on

Example: Do men *open* doors for women?

1 Do women _____ long skirts?
2 Do families _____ their meals together?
3 Do people _____ their doors when they aren't at home?
4 Do men _____ hats when they go out?
5 Do families _____ games together in the evening?
6 Do people _____ at home in the evening?
7 Do people _____ their shoes and _____ slippers when they go into a house?

2 In pairs, ask the questions and answer about people and families you know.

Reading

3 Read the article and match the paragraphs with the pictures.

Example: 1 – C

4 Read again and answer true (T) or false (F).

Example: In some countries, people still throw shoes at the bride at her wedding. **F**

1 All soldiers in the Roman army wore the same sandals.
2 People used to wear high heels and platform shoes many years ago.
3 Everyone wore red shoes when they visited King Louis XIV.
4 At Anglo-Saxon weddings, the groom touched the bride's head with his shoes.

Shoes

Customs and traditions around the world

Perhaps you don't think about shoes very often. Perhaps you think shoes are boring, but shoes have a very interesting history.

(1) A long time ago, people used to throw shoes at the bride and groom after the wedding because they thought it was good luck. Some people still tie shoes to the back of the married couple's car.

(2) In ancient Rome, a soldier's sandals used to tell everyone how important he was in the army – a captain or a foot soldier.

(3) High heels and platform shoes are not new. Hundreds of years ago, people used to wear them in the street because the streets were full of rubbish. The rubbish didn't touch their feet so their feet didn't get dirty.

(4) In France when Louis XIV was king, they thought red shoes were very special. Only the very rich aristocracy used to wear them when they visited the king.

(5) Strange things happened at Anglo-Saxon weddings. The bride's father used to give his daughter's shoes to the groom. Then the groom used to touch the bride's head with these shoes. This meant that the father no longer owned his daughter – she now belonged to the groom.

Grammar focus

5 Look at the examples below and <u>underline</u> the correct words in these explanations.

1 We use *used to* + infinitive to talk about something which happened in the past and *still happens* / *doesn't happen* in the present.
2 We can't use *used to* to talk about something which happened *only once* / *more than once*.

used to	Past simple
(?) What *did* they *use to do* at weddings?	What *did* they *do* at your wedding?
(+) They *used to throw* shoes at the bride.	They *threw* rice over me.
(–) Poor people *didn't use to wear* red shoes.	I *didn't wear* white shoes.

6 🔊 **Listen and repeat the sentences. Pay attention to the pronunciation of *used to*.**

Practice

7 Complete the sentences with the correct form of *used to* and a verb from the box.

wear (x2)   drink   play   go   open   eat

Example: In the UK in the 1920s, most people *didn't use to drink* (not) coffee but now a lot of people do.

1 _____ men _____ doors for women in your country fifty years ago?
2 People _____ (not) in restaurants as often as they do now.
3 When you were young, _____ you _____ a hat and tie when you went out?
4 Fifty years ago, a young man and woman _____ (not) for walks alone together. But that's all changed now.
5 We always _____ shoes when I was a child. Now a lot of children wear trainers.
6 _____ your parents _____ games with you when you were young?

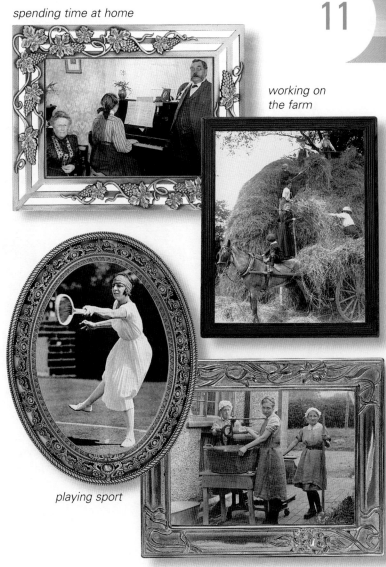

spending time at home

working on the farm

playing sport

doing the housework

Get talking

8 In pairs, discuss how things have changed.

1 Look at the photos above and talk about past customs in Britain.
2 Were these customs the same for people where you come from?
3 What other customs have changed? Think about:
- clothes
- entertainment
- food and drink
- politeness
- family life
- holidays

Language to go

A: Did **women** use to wear **jeans?**
B: No. They always used to wear **dresses.**

> GRAMMAR REFERENCE PAGE 112
> PRACTICE PAGE 95

Vocabulary   Shops and purchases
Grammar   *Because, for* and infinitive of purpose (with *to*)
Language to go   Giving reasons

Win some, lose some

Double or quits

IMAGINE GOING shopping and not paying a penny! If you play double or quits, perhaps you can. Ask the manager if you can throw a coin and say heads or tails. If you lose, you pay double, but if you win, you pay nothing! The *Daily Mail* sent Sarah Ivens to try her luck in various shops.

Vocabulary and speaking

1   **Match the place names with photos from the newspaper article.**

Example: a newsagent's – *A*

1 a convenience store
2 a chemist's
3 a café
4 a restaurant
5 a hairdresser's
6 a clothes shop

2   **In groups, discuss which places you go to for the following. (You can get some things in more than one place.)**

- a cup of coffee
- a haircut
- a can of beer
- medicine
- perfume
- sandwiches
- socks
- a T-shirt
- crisps
- a wash and blow dry
- cigarettes
- toothbrushes
- a newspaper
- matches
- sunglasses
- clothes

3   **Listen and repeat. Put the plurals in the correct sound group.**

grapes / bananas	oranges
socks	sandwiches

Reading and listening

4   **Read the newspaper article above and choose a) or b).**

1 The title means the customer paid:
   a) half the shop price for each thing
   b) twice the shop price or nothing

2 This was possible because the customer:
   a) had a lot of money   b) played a game

5   **Listen to Sarah describing her shopping trip. Did she have more money at the beginning or the end of the trip?**

6   **Listen again and match the places with the totals.**

Example: *1 – d)*

1 newsagent's
2 café
3 clothes shop
4 convenience store
5 chemist's
6 hairdresser's
7 restaurant

a) −£37.50
b) +£4.43
c) −£38.56
d)   +50p
e) +£19.43
f) +£2.50
g) −£35.57

Grammar focus

7 **Look at the examples below and complete these explanations with** *because*, *for* **or** *the infinitive of purpose.*

1 _____ is always followed by a noun.
2 _____ is usually followed by a clause.
3 _____ is sometimes followed by a noun.

Giving reasons	
I went to the café	*because* I wanted a coffee.
	for a coffee.
	to get a coffee.
	to relax.

Practice

8 **Rewrite the sentences using the structures suggested in brackets.**

Example: She went on holiday because she wanted a rest. (for)
She went on holiday for a rest.

1 He phoned the dentist to get an appointment. (for)
2 He joined the club because he wanted to make new friends. (infinitive)
3 They bought some meat because they wanted it for dinner. (for)
4 I stopped at the garage to buy some petrol. (because)
5 We bought some paint because we wanted to paint the chairs. (infinitive)
6 I bought some stamps to put in my stamp album. (for)
7 She came into the living room to get a chair. (because)
8 They went to the sports centre because they wanted to play badminton. (infinitive)

Get talking

9 **Play double or quits for your shopping.**

1 Before you play, complete this form.

FIVE THINGS I BOUGHT LAST MONTH		
shop /place	purchase	price (in local currency)
Example: newsagent's	magazine	$2.40

2 In pairs, ask and answer about your purchases. Ask your partner:
- where he / she went and why
- how much each purchase cost
- how much he / she spent in total

3 In pairs, play double or quits and see who does better.

> GRAMMAR REFERENCE PAGE 112
> PRACTICE PAGE 95

Vocabulary   Large numbers; hotel facilities
Grammar   *Have* and *have got*
Language to go   Facilities and regular activities

The Ritz

Vocabulary

1 📼 **Listen and tick (✓) the numbers that you hear.**

80	300	30	15	18
1,001	41	115	1,500	
700	335	285		
4,000,000	34	60,000		

2 **Listen again and repeat. When do we use *and* in large numbers?**

Reading

3 **Look at the photos and <u>underline</u> what you think are the correct answers.**

Example:
How many guests does the Ritz have each year?
a) <u>60,000</u>   b) 4,000,000

1 How many rooms has it got?
  a) 115   b) 1,001
2 How much is a superior single room per night?
  a) £295   b) £1,500
3 How much is a two-bedroom suite per night?
  a) £80   b) £1,650
4 How much is a short break?
  a) £370   b) £700
5 How much is dinner per person?
  a) £44   b) £385

4 **Read the hotel leaflet and check.**

THE RITZ HOTEL FIRST OPENED ITS DOORS ON THURSDAY 24TH MAY, 1906. WE NOW HAVE, ON AVERAGE, 60,000 GUESTS A YEAR, WHO COME TO STAY IN THE 115 ROOMS AND 18 SUITES; MANY OTHERS ENJOY OUR MEETING ROOMS, BAR AND SPLENDID RESTAURANTS.

ROOM RATES AS OF 5TH MAY:		
	FROM £295	SUPERIOR SINGLE
	FROM £415	DELUXE KING
	FROM £755	SUITE
	FROM £1,650	TWO-BEDROOM SUITE

SHORT BREAKS: ONE NIGHT WITH CHAMPAGNE, FRUIT AND FLOWERS ON ARRIVAL AND FULL ENGLISH BREAKFAST FOR TWO PEOPLE, FROM £370

DINING AND ENTERTAINMENT:	ENGLISH BREAKFAST £22.50
	LUNCH £35
	AFTERNOON TEA £28
	DINNER £44
	DINNER DANCE £59.00

This is a fantastic hotel. The TV in our room's got 30 channels so the kids are happy. We have breakfast in bed every morning so we're happy too. It's got an excellent fitness centre and a wonderful restaurant and room for tea, and it's got a babysitting service too. What more could you want? We're so busy in the hotel that we haven't got time to see London! Love, Jenny, Mark and kids.

Peter Woodley,
10 Weston Road,
Christchurch,
NEW ZEALAND

THE RITZ, London, 150 Piccadilly, London W1J 9BR
Tel: 020 7493 8181 Fax: 020 7493 2687 http://www.theritzlondon.com

Grammar focus

7 **Look at the examples below and complete these explanations with *have* or *have got*.**

1 For possessions, we use _____ or _____ .
2 For routines and regular activites, we only use _____ .

have	have got
(+) It *has* 115 rooms.	It *'s got* 115 rooms.
It *has* 60,000 guests every year.	~~It *'s got* 60,000 guests every year.~~
We *have* breakfast in bed.	~~We *'ve got* breakfast in bed.~~
(−) We *don't have* time to see London.	We *haven't got* time to see London.
(?) *Do* you *have* a fitness centre?	*Have* you *got** a fitness centre?
(Yes, we *do*. / No, we *don't*.)	(Yes, we *have*. / No, we *haven't*.)

* In American English, people usually use *Do you have ...?*

Practice

8 **Complete with the correct form of *have* or *have got*. Give two alternatives where possible.**

1 A: Which hotels in London <u>have / have got</u> fitness centres?
  B: The Ritz _____ one but I don't know about the others.
2 A: Which country _____ 58 McDonald's restaurants?
  B: I don't know, but we _____ (not) any where we live.
3 A: _____ this store _____ more than a million customers a year?
  B: Yes, I think it _____ .
4 How many guests _____ breakfast in their rooms?
5 Which city _____ 73 underground stations?
6 The hotel _____ (not) a sauna.
7 A: Which airline _____ 1,000,000 passengers each month?
  B: Well, I know Rogan Air _____ (not) that many.
8 Which restaurant chain _____ restaurants in 119 countries?

Get talking

9 **In groups, do a quiz.**

   Group A: Turn to page 84.
   Group B: Turn to page 86.

5 **Read the postcard from a guest at the Ritz and answer the questions.**

1 Why are the children happy?
2 Why are the parents happy?
3 Why haven't they seen much of London?

6 **Complete these sentences from the postcard.**

1 It _____ an excellent fitness centre.
2 We _____ breakfast in bed every morning.

Language to go

A: What exercise equipment has the hotel got?
B: I don't know. I just have saunas.

> GRAMMAR REFERENCE PAGE 112
> PRACTICE PAGE 96

Vocabulary   Food and drink
Grammar   *Some, any, much, many, a lot of*
Language to go   Discussing what you eat and drink

Food for thought

Vocabulary and speaking

1   Match the words with the photos.

Example: chocolate – M

1	vegetables	7	fruit
2	onions	8	oranges
3	bread	9	salt
4	cookies	10	juice
5	strawberries	11	water
6	lettuce	12	yoghurt

2   🔊 Listen and repeat. Be careful – the sounds and spelling are not always the same.

3   In pairs, discuss the food in Exercise 1.

1   Which food do you like / dislike?
2   Which food is good / bad for you?

Reading and listening

4   Read about the radio programme 'Food for Thought!'. Is it about:

a) healthy food?
b) cooking?
c) intelligence?

Radio 4

6.00 p.m. FOOD FOR THOUGHT!
Listen to the latest evidence on health and nutrition, and find out what we should and shouldn't eat!

Is this food good or bad for you?	1 What do you think? Why?	2 What does the radio presenter say?	3 Why?
chocolate	bad (bad for your teeth, makes you fat)	good	live longer
salt			
bread			
potatoes			
fruit			
coffee			
tea			

5   Look at the table. In the first column, write *good* or *bad* and give your reasons.

6   🔊 Listen to the programme and write *good* or *bad* in column 2 of the table.

7   Listen again and complete column 3 of the table.

Practice

9 <u>Underline</u> the correct words in the sentences.

1 A: Do you drink <u>*much*</u> / *many* tea?
  B: No, but I drink *much* / *a lot of* coffee.
2 A: Do you eat *much* / *many* vegetables?
  B: Yes, I eat *much* / *a lot of* potatoes every day. I always have some for lunch.
3 A: Do you buy *much* / *many* fruit?
  B: Yes. On Saturdays, I always buy *a lot of* / *many* fruit at the market. I don't buy any in the supermarket.
4 A: How *much* / *many* tomatoes do you usually put in a salad?
  B: Not *much* / *many* – just one or two.
5 A: How *much* / *many* money do you spend on food every week?
  B: Not *much* / *many*, because I live on my own.

10 In pairs, take turns to start each dialogue from Exercise 9 and give answers that are true for you.

Get talking

11 Talk about your typical diet.

1 Individually, write down the food you usually have for breakfast, lunch and dinner. Think about:
  • how much you eat of each thing
  • how good or bad it is for you

2 In groups, tell other students what you eat. Discuss what's good and bad about it. Who has the healthiest diet?

Language to go

A: Do you eat much fruit?
B: Yes, I eat a lot of fruit but I don't eat many vegetables.

Grammar focus

8 Look at the examples below and choose a) or b) to complete these explanations.

1 We generally use _____ to talk about a large quantity.
  a) *some* / *any* b) *much* / *many* / *a lot of*

2 We use _____ with countable nouns (e.g. *potatoes*) and _____ with uncountable nouns (e.g. *bread*).
  a) *much* / *a lot of* b) *many* / *a lot of*

Quantifiers + countable / uncountable nouns

some / *any*
(+) Have *some* bread / potatoes.
(–) Don't have *any* tea / cookies.
(?) Do you have *any* salt / cookies?

much / *many* / *a lot of*
(+) Eat *a lot of* fruit / vegetables.
(–) Don't eat *much* chocolate / *many* cookies.
(?) How *much* bread | can you eat?
    How *many* potatoes |

> GRAMMAR REFERENCE PAGE 112
> PRACTICE PAGE 96

LESSON **15**
Modals

Vocabulary British and American words for clothes
Grammar Present and past obligation with *have* / *had to*
Language to go Talking about obligation

A nice place to work

Vocabulary and speaking

1 Match an American and a British word with each picture.

Example: 1 – 9 – E

American English   **British English**

1 sneakers   6 waistcoat

2 sweater   7 jumper

3 vest   8 vest

4 pants   9 trainers

5 undershirt   10 trousers

2 **In pairs, rewrite this dialogue in British English. Then practise the dialogue.**

A: Hi. I'm looking for some pants to go with my favourite sweater.

B: How about these? They look great with sneakers.

A: I don't know. I don't often wear sneakers ...

B: Or these? They come with a free vest.

A: Thanks. I'll try them on. And do you have any undershirts?

B: Yes, of course. You'll find some over there.

3 **Describe the clothes the people are wearing in the photo.**

Listening

4 🔲 **Listen and answer true (T) or false (F).**

Example:
Tom Banks works in New York. *T*

1 He works in a bank.
2 He wears a suit for work.
3 In 1996 the company started dressdown days on Fridays.
4 No one wears suits.
5 He likes dressdown.
6 He has to call the Managing Director 'Sir'.
7 He can work at different times each day.
8 He can work at home sometimes.

Grammar focus

5 **Look at the examples below and match one to each of these meanings.**

1 It isn't necessary.
2 It is necessary.
3 It wasn't necessary.
4 It was necessary.

---

have / had to (obligation)

Present
(+) We *have to wear* clothes that look good.
(–) You *don't have to wear* casual clothes.
(?) *Does* everyone *have to wear* office casual?
(Yes, they *do.* / No, they *don't.*)

Past
(+) We *had to wear* suits every day.
(–) We *didn't have to wear* suits on Fridays.
(?) *Did* they *have to wear* suits before 1996?
(Yes, they *did.* / No, they *didn't.*)

Practice

6 **Write sentences using the correct form of *have to*.**

Example: call the managers 'Mr' and 'Miss' (necessary?)
(she) <u>Does she have to call the managers 'Mr' and 'Miss'?</u>

1 work from 9 a.m. to 5 p.m. (not necessary)
You _____ .
2 wear formal clothes before 1996 (necessary?)
(they) _____ ?
3 carry a mobile phone at all times (necessary)
He _____ .
4 wear smart clothes (not necessary)
She _____ .
5 speak many languages (necessary?)
(you) _____ ?
6 go to the office every day last year (not necessary)
We _____ .
7 arrive early yesterday morning (necessary)
They _____ .
8 have a computer at home (necessary?)
(I) _____ ?

Get talking ...

7 **In pairs, talk about what is necessary and not necessary in the place where you work or study. Has it always been this way? Think about:**

• clothes
• what you call your clients / colleagues / teachers
• the times you work or study
• where you work or study

... and writing

8 **Write to an English friend who is coming to work in an office in your country. Tell him / her about work practices. Think about:**

• clothes • hours of work • meals • length of breaks

Begin your letter:

Dear Barbara / Nick,

Here is the information that you wanted about working in ...

Language to go

A: A meeting at the embassy! Do I have to wear something smart?
B: No, you don't. But you have to be there before 8 p.m.

> GRAMMAR REFERENCE PAGE 113
> PRACTICE PAGE 97

Vocabulary   Topics for TV soaps
Grammar   Future predictions with *will* / *won't*
Language to go   Predicting the future

Mumbai Soap

Reading and speaking

1   Answer these questions.

1 Do you like watching soaps?
2 Which soaps do you watch or know about?
3 Which of these topics does your favourite soap often include?
   • love   • sport
   • marriage   • travel
   • crime   • family life

2   Read part 1 of 'Mumbai Soap'. What is Mina's problem?

3   Decide what you think Mina will do. Choose a), b) or c) and say why.

   a) She'll run away and marry Sanjay.
   b) She'll accept the husband her parents have chosen.
   c) She'll go to London.

4   Read part 2 of the story and check your predictions.

5   Decide what you think will happen next. Choose a), b) or c) and say why.

   a) Mina will go back to India and Sanjay.
   b) She'll accept the job but she won't marry Ravi.
   c) She'll accept the job and marry Ravi.

6   Read part 3 of the story and check your predictions.

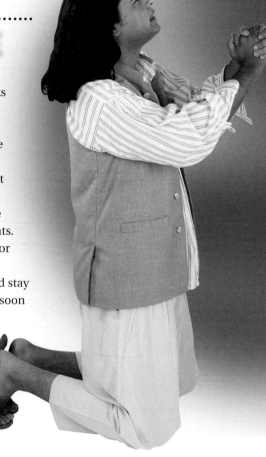

....
PART ONE

'MINA, you can't leave me,' cries Sanjay, and Mina thinks her heart will break. She thinks about the cricket match in Mumbai where she first met Sanjay. She knows her parents will never accept this man with no money or family connections. And she loves and respects her parents. 'We have found a husband for you,' they say. 'You must get married or go to London and stay with our family there. You'll soon forget Sanjay.'

Listening

7   📼 Listen to the story so far. In groups, discuss how you think the story will end.

Grammar focus

8   Look at the examples below and <u>underline</u> the correct words in these explanations.

1 We use *will* or *won't* to make predictions based on *personal opinion* / *factual information*.
2 We use *think + won't* / *don't think + will* to make negative predictions.

Future predictions	
will / *won't*	*think* / *don't think + will*
(+) You *'ll* (*will*) soon *forget* him.	She *thinks* her heart *will break*.
(–) She *won't* (*will not*) *marry* anyone else.	I *don't think* I*'ll see* her again.
(?) *Will* we *meet* again?	*Do* you *think* it *'ll be* too late?

9   📼 Listen and repeat the sentences. Pay attention to the contracted forms.

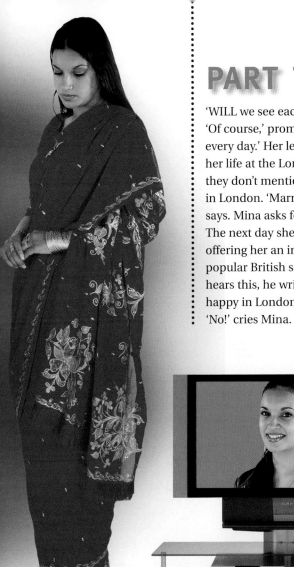

PART TWO

'WILL we see each other again?' asks Sanjay. 'Of course,' promises Mina. 'And I'll write every day.' Her letters tell Sanjay all about her life at the London drama school. But they don't mention Ravi, a family friend in London. 'Marry me, Mina,' Ravi says. Mina asks for time to think. The next day she gets a letter offering her an important role in a popular British soap. When Sanjay hears this, he writes, 'I know you are happy in London. Please forget me.' 'No!' cries Mina.

PART THREE

FIVE years later, Sanjay turns on the TV in his London hotel room. Tomorrow he will play cricket for India. He knows Mina is in London but he doesn't think he'll see her again. He still remembers her last letter: 'I won't marry anyone else but I must stay in London. It's not just the job ... it's also my family. I'll always love you.' Sanjay can hear her voice. He turns in surprise and sees her on the TV screen. 'She's as beautiful as ever. Is it too late?' he asks himself.

Practice

10 **Complete the TV guide text below with *will* or *won't* and a verb from the box. How similar were your predictions in Exercise 7?**

> get   have to   phone   go   meet
> speak   recognise   happen   be

What <u>will happen</u> in the final episode of 'Mumbai Soap'?
Sanjay (1) _____ Mina's phone number from a mutual friend. He (2) _____ her but he'll hear a man's voice and he (3) _____ (not). But Mina and Sanjay (4) _____ again. I think Mina (5) _____ to Sanjay's cricket match with friends. I don't think she (6) _____ him at first. But he'll be the hero of the match. Do you think she (7) _____ with Ravi? I can't tell you everything. You (8) _____ watch and find out!

Get talking

11 **In groups, predict the following. Remember to check your predictions next week.**

1 What will happen in the next episode of your favourite soap or TV series?
2 What will be the result of the next big sports event in your area?
3 What will the newspapers' main story be tomorrow?
4 What will the weather be like tomorrow?
5 What will your teacher wear next lesson?

Language to go

A: Will you see her tonight?
B: No, I won't. I don't think I'll ever see her again.

> GRAMMAR REFERENCE PAGE 113
> PRACTICE PAGE 97

Vocabulary   Adjectives describing places and objects; transport
Grammar   Superlatives
Language to go   Using superlatives to describe places

Camden Market

Come to CAMDEN TOWN

London's most popular tourist destination

Why is it the best place to visit?

It's got

- the biggest craft market in London
- the widest selection of second-hand clothes

You'll see

- young people wearing the newest fashions
- the capital's most interesting art in small art galleries and shops

You can

- listen to the most exciting music in town, on the street or in clubs
- eat in the trendiest cafés, bars and restaurants

How do you get here?

Public transport to and from Camden is excellent. It's one of the easiest places to get to in London.

The quickest way is by **tube** to Camden Town from anywhere in London.

Or take a **train** to Camden Road Station. It's direct from many places in north London.

The cheapest way from central London is by **bus**. Take the 23, 27, 29, 134 or 135.

Of course, you can get here by **car**, but parking is very difficult. Or you could take a **taxi** – very expensive!

Vocabulary and speaking

1 Look at the photo and discuss the questions.

1 Have you ever heard of Camden Market?
2 What markets do you know? What's their main attraction?

2 Look again and underline the correct adjectives.

Camden Town is very *popular* / *unpopular* with young people in London. It is special because of its (1) *old-fashioned* / *trendy* market and its (2) *attractive* / *unattractive* canal location. Every Saturday and Sunday, the market is (3) *busy* / *quiet* with both Londoners and tourists. It is particularly (4) *famous* / *unknown* for ethnic handicrafts from all over the world. It also sells cheap (5) *new* / *second-hand* clothes, which are popular with students.

Reading

3 Read the advert and answer the questions.

1 Why is Camden a good place to:
   a) buy clothes?   b) look at art?   c) eat?
2 Why is it good to go by tube?
3 Why is it good to go by bus?
4 How else can you get there?

Grammar focus

4 Look at the examples below and answer these questions.

1 Is there a bigger craft market than Camden?
2 Is there a more popular tourist destination?
3 Is there a better place to visit than Camden?

Superlatives

1-syllable adjectives
Camden has *the biggest* craft market in London.
The quickest way to get there is by tube.

2-syllable adjectives ending in *y*
It's one of *the easiest* places to get to.

2 / 3 / 4-syllable adjectives
It's *the most popular* tourist destination.

Irregular superlatives
good   It's *the best* place to visit.
bad   It's *the worst* place to park.

Practice

5 Make questions using the superlative form of the adjectives.

Example: What / near / form of transport to your home?
What is the nearest form of transport to your home?

1 What / cheap / way for you to come to school (or work)?
2 What / easy / way?
3 What / bad / thing about the journey?
4 What / big / problem with transport where you live?
5 What / interesting / place you have visited recently?
6 What / good / thing about this place?
7 What / popular / tourist destination in your area?
8 What / busy / time to go there?

6 In pairs, ask and answer the questions above.

Get talking ...

7 Talk about your favourite tourist destinations.

1 Work individually or in pairs. Think about the area where you live or another tourist area.
   • What are the best places to visit and the most interesting things you can do there?
   • How do you get there? (the quickest / cheapest forms of transport etc.)

2 Tell other students about the place you chose. Whose place is the most interesting?

... and writing

8 Make an advert for tourists.

Write about your favourite tourist destination. Use the advert for Camden Town as a model.

Language to go

A: **Where's** the nearest restaurant?
B: Over there. It has the best food in town.

> GRAMMAR REFERENCE PAGE 113
> PRACTICE PAGE 98

Vocabulary   Travel: verb + noun combinations
Grammar   Present perfect with *yet* and *already*
Language to go   Saying what you've done so far

On the move

Vocabulary and speaking

1 **Look at the things in the picture. Which do / don't you usually take when you travel? What else do you take?**

2 **Match the columns to find the verbs and nouns that go together.**

Example: **1 – b)**

1 Go to the embassy and *get*
2 She'll have to *renew*
3 I'm waiting for the bank to *transfer*
4 Ask the doctor if you need to *have*
5 I'll fold the clothes if you *pack*
6 I'll phone the travel agency and *book*

a) *her passport* soon.
b) *a visa* for the USA.
c) *the (suit)case.*
d) train *tickets* and *a hotel.*
e) *the money.*
f) *a vaccination* against cholera.

- sell the car ✓
- transfer the money
- have my vaccinations
- renew my passport
- get a visa
- book the ticket
- book a hotel room
- pack my cases

Listening

3 🔊 **Listen and <u>underline</u> the correct answers.**

1 When is Mel going to travel?
   a) next week   b) the week after next
2 Where is she going to stay?
   a) in London   b) in Cairo
3 Why is she going to go there?
   a) for a holiday   b) for work

4 **Listen again. Tick (✓) the travel preparations she has completed on the list above.**

Grammar focus

5 **Look at the examples below and complete these explanations with *yet*, *not yet* or *already*.**

When we talk about time up to and including the present moment, we use:

1 _____ when the action is complete.
   (Sometimes we are surprised.)
2 _____ when the action is not complete
   but we think it will happen.
3 _____ to ask if the action is complete.

Present perfect with *yet* and *already*
(?) *Have* you *sold* the car *yet?*
(+) I*'ve already booked* the ticket.
(−) She *hasn't phoned* back *yet.*

Practice

6 **Look at the list from Exercise 4 and write sentences to say what Mel has / hasn't done.**

Example: *She's already sold the car.*

7 **In pairs, compare your answers. Take turns to ask and answer.**

Example:
A: *Has she sold the car yet?*
B: *Yes, she has. / No, not yet.*

Get talking

8 **You and two colleagues are going abroad together. Talk about your preparations.**

1 Read the lists. Each person in your group should take responsibility for one list.

2 Individually, look at your list and tick two things you have already done.

3 In your group, find out which things your colleagues have already done. Make a list of all the things left to do. Discuss who is going to do each one and when.

LIST A
- renew the passports
- get the visas
- change some money
- pack your case

LIST B
- book a hotel for the first night
- rent a car
- get an international driver's licence
- pack your case

LIST C
- book ferry tickets for you and the car
- buy a good guide book
- organise travel insurance
- pack your case

Language to go

A: Have you booked the tickets yet?
B: No, I've already told you, I haven't done that yet.

> GRAMMAR REFERENCE PAGE 113
> PRACTICE PAGE 98

LESSON 19
Functions

Vocabulary   Sports: word building
Function   Past ability with *could* and *be good at*
Language to go   Talking about how well you could do things

Real fighters

Vocabulary and speaking

1   Complete the table.

Person	Sport	Verb
boxer	boxing	*to box*
	fighting	to fight
swimmer		
cyclist		to cycle
	running	
		to dance
skier		

2   In pairs, find out if your partner can *box*, *swim*, *cycle*, *dance* or *ski*. How well can they do each activity?

Example:
A: *Can you ski?*
B: *Yes, I can.*
A: *How well can you ski?*
B: *Very well / quite well / not very well.*

Reading

3   Look at the photos and try to answer the questions.

1 Who are the two boxers?
2 What's the connection between them?
3 When did each one start boxing?
4 Whose career has been more successful?

4   Now read and check your answers.

5   Read again and complete the table about Muhammad Ali.

	he could	he couldn't
Before his illness	swim	✕
After his illness		

THE GREATEST

LAILA ALI is Muhammad Ali's daughter. In 1999, at the age of twenty, Laila began boxing. In two years, she won seven fights and showed she could box quite well. But she couldn't beat her father's reputation.

Language focus

6   Look at the examples below and match the two halves of these explanations.

1 *Could / couldn't* is followed by
2 *Was / were good at* is followed by

a) a noun or *-ing* form.
b) an infinitive (without *to*).

Past ability

could / couldn't

(+++)	Ali *could*		*really well.*
(++)	They *could*		*well.*
(+)	Laila *could*	box	*quite well.*
(−)	We *couldn't*		*very well.*
(−−)	He *couldn't*		*at all.*

was / were good at

(+++)	Ali *was really*		
(++)	They *were*		
(+)	Laila *was quite*	*good at*	*sport.*
(−)	We *weren't very*		*boxing.*
(−−)	He *was no*		

MUHAMMAD ALI was 'The Greatest'. He was the only boxer to become heavyweight champion of the world three times. He was born in 1942 and was called Cassius Clay. He started boxing in 1954. Somebody stole his new bicycle and he wanted to hit the boy who stole it, so he went to a gym to learn how to fight. Ali trained six days a week. He could already swim very well. Now he ran, skipped and boxed. He was soon really good at boxing. Clay converted to Islam in 1964 and changed his name to Muhammad Ali.

As he got older, Ali became ill. He couldn't speak very well or move quickly. He was no good at boxing. But he could still help other people to fight for a better world. And after all those years, he still wanted to find and hit the boy who stole his bike. 'That was a good bike,' he said.

Practice

7 Write complete sentences about past ability, using the adverbs suggested in brackets.

Example: Jane / good / yoga so she became a yoga teacher. (+++)
Jane was really good at yoga so she became a yoga teacher.

1 Martin / could / swim so he joined a swimming club. (+)
2 I / good / playing the piano when I was young but now I can play quite well. (– –)
3 They / could / play golf so they decided to have lessons. (–)
4 We / good / dancing so we entered the salsa competition. (++)
5 My brother / good / taking photos so he was very sad when I broke his camera. (+++)
6 She / could / sing before she got ill. (++)
7 He / good / sport so he didn't enjoy games lessons at school. (–)
8 I / could / speak / Italian when I got my first job in Rome. (– –)

Get talking

8 Talk about your abilities ten years ago.

1 Individually, complete your part of the survey form. Write + / – signs to show how well you could do each thing.

PAST ABILITIES SURVEY

Ten years ago, could you ...	YOU How well?	YOUR PARTNER How well?
swim?		
cook?		
drive?		
play an instrument?		
ride a bike?		
speak a foreign language?		
other?		

2 In pairs, ask and answer questions and complete the survey form for your partner.

Example:
A: *Could you swim ten years ago?*
B: *Yes, I could swim well. (++)*
A: *Could you cook?*
B: *No, I couldn't cook at all. (– –)*

3 Report your partner's answers to the class. Which things could everyone in the class do?

Language to go

A: Could you read before you left primary school?
B: I couldn't read very well, but I was really good at fighting.

> GRAMMAR REFERENCE PAGE 113
> PRACTICE PAGE 99

Vocabulary   Adjectives to describe advertised products
Grammar   First conditional (*if* + present simple + *will*)
Language to go   Talking about future possibility

The message behind the ad

Speaking and listening

3 In groups, describe an advert you've seen for the types of product on the left.

4 🔲 Listen to the interview with an advertising executive. Tick (✔) the products that you hear them talk about.

5 Listen again and answer the questions.

1 What kind of people do they use in car adverts?
2 Which products often use families in their adverts?
3 Does the interviewer think that most adverts use sex to sell products?
4 Do people remember adverts for a long time?

Grammar focus

6 **Look at the examples below and <u>underline</u> the correct words in these explanations.**

1 We are talking about *present* / *future* time.
2 The verb in the *if* clause is a *present* / *future* form.
3 The *if* clause *always comes first* / *can come first or second* in the sentence.
4 When the *if* clause comes first, it *is* / *isn't* usually followed by a comma.

First conditional
(+) *If* you *buy* this car, you *'ll meet* a beautiful woman. People *will remember* it *if* it *'s* funny.
(−) Your kids *won't* (*will not*) *get* sunburnt *if* you *use* this suncream.
(?) What *will happen if* I *use* this shampoo?

7 🔲 **Listen and repeat the examples above. Pay attention to intonation.**

Vocabulary

1 **<u>Underline</u> the best adjectives for these products.**

Example: Medallion, a *delicious* / *shiny* new coffee. Try it – you'll love it.

1 You'll have *shiny* / *fresh* hair every time you use Gloss shampoo. So for *reliable* / *healthy-looking* hair, use it today.
2 Sunease suncream will keep your skin *fast* / *safe* from sunburn all through the day. And it keeps your skin *delicious* / *soft* too!
3 Drink *safe* / *fresh* orange juice for breakfast – the *clean* / *healthy* way to start your day.
4 Now Lux-Clean washing powder is even better. Your clothes will always be *clean* / *delicious* and so very *reliable* / *soft*.
5 This new Tomoto sports car is *soft* / *fast* and completely *healthy* / *reliable*.

2 🔲 Listen and check.

Perfume for the confident woman

Cool guy, cool beer

START THE DAY WITH JUICE

Practice

8 **Complete the advert slogans with the correct form of the verbs in brackets.**

Example: You **'ll lose** (lose) weight quickly if you **don't eat** (not eat) sweet things.

1 If you _____ (taste) this fresh Colombian coffee, you _____ (not want) to drink anything else.
2 If you _____ (use) Gloss shampoo, your hair _____ (look) really shiny.
3 You _____ (have) more energy if you _____ (eat) lots of fresh fruit.
4 If anything _____ (go) wrong with this machine, we _____ (repair) it for free.
5 If you _____ (buy) two bottles, you _____ (get) one free.
6 You _____ (not feel) so unhealthy if you _____ (exercise) at our gym every day.
7 Your skin _____ (be) softer if you _____ (wash) with Callon soap every day.

Get talking

9 **Discuss the three adverts above.**

1 In groups, decide who the advertisers are trying to sell the products to.
   • Are they young, middle-aged or old?
   • Are they men or women, or both?
   • Are they single or married people?
   • Do they have children?

2 Use the first conditional to write down the message behind the adverts.

3 Compare what you have written with other groups.

Language to go

A: If you buy this car, you'll get lots of men.
B: Well, I'll certainly need a mechanic!

> GRAMMAR REFERENCE PAGE 114
> PRACTICE PAGE 99

Vocabulary   Irregular verbs
Grammar   Past simple and past continuous
Language to go   Describing past events in stories

The story of Grace

Listening and reading

1 Find these things in picture A.

> deer   country house
> rifle   river   hunter

2 📼 Listen and look at the picture on the right, then answer the questions.

1 Who is Roddy?
2 Why is Grace crying?

3 Read the story and put pictures A – E in order.

Example: 1 – *A*

PART ONE

Twenty years ago, Grace lived in Scotland with her son, Sam. Sam fell in love with Fiona Stewart. Fiona was the daughter of a rich landowner called Jim Stewart. Fiona and Sam were both sixteen and very much in love.

One beautiful summer's day, Sam and Fiona were walking by the river on her father's land. Her father was out hunting deer when he saw the two young lovers. He was furious. Nobody was good enough for his daughter.

'If you see Fiona again, I'll kill you!' he said. And he pointed his rifle at Sam's heart.

PART TWO

That same night, Sam went to see Fiona. He wanted to say to her, 'I don't care what your father says. I love you, Fiona, and I'll wait for you forever.'

When he arrived at the house, Fiona was sitting at her bedroom window, crying. He began to climb the tree outside her room. He was still climbing the tree when Jim Stewart came out of the house with his rifle. Without saying a word, he shot Sam. Sam died.

PART THREE

Jim Stewart told the police, 'I thought he was a burglar. And when I fired my rifle, I wasn't trying to kill him. I only wanted to frighten him.'

Jim Stewart didn't go to prison and he soon left Scotland.

Grace was heartbroken. All the people from the village came to Sam's funeral. Everyone loved Grace and Sam, and everyone hated Jim Stewart.

PART FOUR

No one knew where Jim Stewart was until last night. After twenty years he came back to Scotland. He was driving to his country house when his car suddenly stopped. He walked to the nearest village and found a little hotel. It was Grace's hotel. He went in. He didn't know who Grace was, but Grace immediately knew who he was. He asked Grace for a room and a glass of whisky.

PART FIVE

Grace carried the whisky to his room.

Grammar focus

4 **Look at the examples below and <u>underline</u> the correct words in these explanations.**

1 The action in a) started *before* / *after* the action in b).
2 The action that started first *was* / *wasn't* finished before the second action started.

Past simple (a)	Past continuous (b)
(+) When Sam *arrived*,	Fiona *was sitting* at the window.
(−) When I *fired* my rifle,	I *wasn't trying* to kill him.
(?) When Mr Stewart *came out*,	what *was* Sam *doing*?

5 📼 **Listen and practise the weak forms of *was* and *were*.**

1 Grace was working at home.
2 We were having lunch.
3 They were walking by the river.
4 He was standing near the window.

Practice

6 **Complete each sentence using one past simple and one past continuous form.**

Example:
When Sam / meet / Fiona for the first time, she / ride / her horse.
When Sam met Fiona for the first time, she was riding her horse.

1 When Jim Stewart / see / Sam and Fiona, they / walk / by the river.
2 Fiona / cry / in her bedroom when Sam / arrive / at the house.
3 When Jim Stewart / come / out with a rifle, who / climb / the tree?
4 Grace / work / in the garden when Roddy / tell / her about her son.
5 Where / Jim Stewart / sit / when Grace / give / him the whisky?
6 What / Roddy / do / when Grace / run / into the police station?

Get talking

7 **Tell the end of the story.**

Group A: Turn to page 84.
Group B: Turn to page 87.

Language to go

A: What was she doing when he arrived?
B: She was crying.

> GRAMMAR REFERENCE PAGE 114
> PRACTICE PAGE 100

Vocabulary Jobs
Grammar *Like + -ing* and *would like* and infinitive with (*to*)
Language to go Talking about career preferences

Just the job for you

Vocabulary

1 **Look at the photos and describe the jobs with these phrases.**

Example: *A farmer works outside.*

- work outside
- work inside
- earn a good salary
- travel a lot
- work with people
- work with animals
- work with machines
- work alone
- be creative
- be active
- have a lot of responsibility

farmer

barman

chef

mechanic

market researcher

airline pilot

1 **Do you like creating new menus?**
Would you like to join a new catering company?
We cater for weddings, parties and business conferences.

2
☐ Have you got a good telephone voice?
☐ Would you like to work from home?
☐ Would you like to choose what time you work?

We need people to conduct phone interviews about products for an advertising agency.

3 Do you like learning new skills?
Would you like to work with cars and motorbikes?
Our motor repairs business offers young people on-the-job training.

4 Do you like working with people? Would you like to work in a busy nightclub?
Then we need you for a new club that's opening soon in MANHATTAN.

Reading and speaking

2 **Read the adverts and match them with jobs from Exercise 1.**

Example: 1 – *chef*

3 **Read the adverts again and choose:**

1 a job you would like to do
2 a job you wouldn't like to do

4 **In pairs, discuss why you chose or didn't choose each job.**

Grammar focus

5 **Look at the examples below and decide which verb, *like* or *would like*, is:**

1 imagining a future possibility.
2 talking about present likes and dislikes.

like + *-ing* form	*would like to* + infinitive
(?) *Do* you *like working* with people? (Yes, I *do*. / No, I *don't*.)	*Would* you *like to work* from home? (Yes, I *would*. / No, I *wouldn't*.)
(+) I *like learning* new skills.	I'*d like to be* a mechanic.
(–) I *don't like working* outside.	I *wouldn't like to be* a farmer.

Practice

6 **A careers officer (A) is talking to a student (B). Underline and correct the mistakes.**

A: So, what type of job <u>do</u> you like to have?   Example: <u>would</u>
B: I've been a barman, which is fun. I like to working   1 _____
   with people. But I'd also like earn some good money. 2 _____
A: And your brother? What job would he liking to do?   3 _____
B: Well, he likes to working outside and he loves   4 _____
   animals, so he'd likes to be a farmer. He'd like to   5 _____
   share a farm with me, but I don't know. I liking   6 _____
   being outside but I not would want to work outside 7 _____
   all the time. My perfect job? I'd like be a   8 _____
   pilot. I like travelling and I'd like to visiting cities 9 _____
   all over the world. I really like to learn to fly.   10 _____

7 🎧 **Listen and check.**

Get talking ...

8 **Help your partner to choose a new career.**

1 Write down three jobs you would like to do and three jobs you wouldn't like to do. Keep this until later.

2 Ask your partner questions using vocabulary from Exercise 1.

  Do you like ... ?
  Would you like to ... ?

3 Write down three jobs you think your partner would like to do and three he / she wouldn't like to do.

4 Compare your list with the list your partner made.

... and writing

9 **Look again at the adverts above. Write a similar advert for a job you would like to do.**

Language to go

A: Do you like working here?
B: No, I don't.
A: Would you like to work abroad?
B: Yes, I would.

> GRAMMAR REFERENCE PAGE 114
> PRACTICE PAGE 100

Vocabulary	Materials and possessions
Grammar	Present simple passive
Language to go	Describing the origins of products

Made in the USA

Vocabulary and speaking

1 Match the materials in the box with objects on the poster.

> wood   silver   leather
> cotton   glass   metal
> lycra   gold

Example: F – *leather sandals*

2 In pairs, talk about materials.

1 Name as many things as you can made of wood or glass.
2 Do you prefer silver or gold jewellery?
3 Do you wear more cotton or lycra?
4 Have you got any leather clothes?
5 What's your favourite possession made of metal?
6 What's your most expensive possession? What material is it?

Visit Fisherman's Wharf
with its spectacular view of the bay and handicrafts from all over the world

Listening

3  Listen to Rachel and Simon, British tourists at Fisherman's Wharf in San Francisco. What does Simon buy and why?

4 Listen again and complete the table for the objects they talk about.

	Object	Material	Country of origin	Price
1	earrings			
2				
3				

Grammar focus

5 Look at the examples below and answer these questions.

1 Which is more important in the passive sentences?
   a) the boxes and silver
   b) the people who make, sell or buy them
2 How do we form the present passive?
   a) be + past participle   b) do + infinitive

Present simple (passive and active)

Passive	Active
Where *are* they *made*?	Where *do* they *make* them?
What *are* they *made of*?	What *do* they *make* them *of*?
The boxes *are made in* Hungary.	They *make* the boxes *in* Hungary.
All my silver *is bought in* Mexico.	I *buy* all my silver *in* Mexico.

Practice

6 Complete the sentences with the active or passive form of the verbs in brackets.

Example: My favourite shorts <u>are made</u> (make) of lycra.

1 They _____ (make) good leather shoes in Brazil.
2 A lot of jewellery _____ (sell) at the market.
3 _____ (these gloves make) in Italy?
4 She _____ (not buy) all her clothes in France.
5 _____ (they sell) cigarettes in that shop?
6 This newspaper _____ (buy) by people interested in business.
7 This watch _____ (not make) of real gold.
8 I'm sure these chairs _____ (make) of wood.

Get talking

7 **In pairs, describe objects for your partner to guess.**

Student A: Turn to page 84.
Student B: Turn to page 87.

Language to go

A: Did you make that ring?
B: Yes, I did.
A: What's it made of?
B: Silver.

> GRAMMAR REFERENCE PAGE 114
> PRACTICE PAGE 101

Vocabulary   The theatre
Grammar   *A / an* and *the*
Language to go   Talking about a theatre show

A long run

Vocabulary and speaking

1 <u>Underline</u> the best words for these sentences.

Example:
The Globe is the name of a
theatre / *playwright* in
London.

1 In an *opera* / *musical*, many words are spoken as well as sung.
2 A *play* / *game* is performed by actors.
3 The *spectators* / *audience* clap at the end of the play.
4 The *singer* / *composer* writes the music.
5 The most expensive *seats* / *chairs* are at the front of the theatre.

2 In pairs, discuss these questions.

1 Do you prefer going to the theatre or cinema? Why?
2 What is the most expensive seat you have ever had at the theatre or cinema?
3 Can you name any famous musicals?
4 Who is your country's most famous playwright?
5 Who is your favourite composer?
6 Do you enjoy reading plays?

Long Theatre runs in London

The Mousetrap

AGATHA CHRISTIE'S most famous murder mystery is the world's longest-running play. 'The Mousetrap' opened in 1952, and more than ten million people have seen it.

In the play, a man and his wife have an old house. They turn the house into a small hotel. After some guests arrive, it snows and nobody can leave. A police officer arrives and says one of the people in the house is a murderer. During the play, the audience tries to work out who the murderer is.

So what makes this more popular than other murder mysteries? Well, the play has a very surprising ending and the murderer asks the audience to keep it a secret. Amazingly they do – so if you want to know who did it, you have to go and see the play!

Phantom of the Opera

ANDREW LLOYD WEBBER is the

(continued on page 87)

Reading

3 **Read about one play only and complete your part of the table.**

Student A: Read about 'The Mousetrap', above.
Student B: Turn to page 87 and read about 'Phantom of the Opera'.

		The Mousetrap	Phantom of the Opera
1	date of first performance	1952	1986
2	type of show		
3	how it ends		
4	reasons for popularity		

4 **Ask your partner about his / her play and complete the table.**

The PHANTOM of the OPERA

Grammar focus

5 Look at the examples below and complete these explanations with *a / an* or *the*.

We generally use:

1 _____ the first time we talk about something.

2 _____ when we talk about the same thing again.

3 _____ when there is only one.

4 _____ with superlative adjectives.

a / an	the
A young couple have *an* old house.	They turn *the* house into a small hotel. You have to go and see *the* play. 'The Mousetrap' is *the* longest running play.
He falls in love with *an* opera singer.	*The* opera singer loves Raoul. *The* Phantom is a young composer. 'Phantom of the Opera' is *the* most successful musical.

6 Listen and repeat the examples above.

1 How do we say *a* and *the* before a consonant?

2 How do we say *an* and *the* before a vowel?

Practice

7 Complete each gap with *a / an* or *the*.

'Romeo and Juliet' is <u>the</u> most popular of Shakespeare's plays. (1) _____ story is about (2) _____ young woman and (3) _____ young man who fall in love. (4) _____ young man is called Romeo and (5) _____ young woman is called Juliet. Their families are enemies so they marry in secret. Romeo gets into a fight and kills (6) _____ young man. (7) _____ young man is Juliet's cousin. Romeo has to leave (8) _____ city. Juliet sends him (9) _____ message. (10) _____ message is very important because it explains how they can stay together. But Romeo doesn't get it. Because of this, Romeo and Juliet both kill themselves at (11) _____ end of (12) _____ play.

Get writing

8 Write the story of the musical 'West Side Story', using the prompts below and the text in Exercise 7 as a model.

- modern-day 'Romeo and Juliet' in New York
- young man (Tony) / fall in love / young woman (Maria)
- Tony / in a street gang (the Jets)
- Maria's brother / in another street gang (the Sharks)
- Jets / Sharks / enemies
- Jets / Sharks / fight
- a Jet / kill / Maria's brother
- then a Shark / kill / Tony

Language to go

A: I saw a play last night.

B: What was it like?

A: The play was good but the acting was awful.

> GRAMMAR REFERENCE PAGE 114

> PRACTICE PAGE 101

Vocabulary   Verb + noun combinations
Grammar   *Have to, don't have to, mustn't*
Language to go   Expressing obligation and prohibition

Smart agreements

'Love me forever ... or pay 5 million dollars!'

NO ONE with big money in California or New York these days gets married without a pre-nuptial agreement. This is particularly true for Hollywood actors, who agree, for example, that a husband or wife will receive $5 million if their partner is unfaithful. But these agreements are also becoming popular in European countries such as Germany and the Netherlands. Australia, too, now accepts them.

Bus driver Bruce Collins, from Perth, is delighted. His girlfriend

Suzanne Taylor has asked him to marry her. Bruce has agreed but plans to sign a pre-nuptial

agreement first. 'Suzanne mustn't cut her hair short and she mustn't stay out late,' he told us. 'Last year she forgot the anniversary of the day we met and then she lost her temper. She definitely mustn't do that again.'

Suzanne thinks he's making a fuss over nothing. 'He'll have a good life. I haven't got a job so I can stay at home all day. In the agreement it says that he doesn't have to do much housework. He doesn't have to do the cooking. All he has to do is the washing up.'

But Bruce has a surprise for Suzanne. 'There's one thing in the agreement that she doesn't know about yet. Before I marry Suzanne, she has to ... get a job!'

Vocabulary and speaking

1 **Match the columns to find the verbs and nouns that go together.**

Example: **1 – f)**

1 I can't get into the house. I've *lost*
2 I'm tired. I'm not going to *stay*
3 He always shouts when he *loses*
4 I hate dirty dishes! Please *do*
5 She hates complaining or *making*
6 She does it every year! She *forgot*
7 This flat is so dirty. We should *do*
8 He can't change his mind.
   We *made*

a) *our anniversary* again.
b) *a fuss* in restaurants.
c) *the washing up* soon.
d) *an agreement*.
e) *some housework*.
f) *my key*.
g) *his temper*.
h) *out late* tonight.

2 **In pairs, talk about the last time you did three of the things above.**

Example: **I lost my keys last month and I couldn't get into my house.**

Reading

3 **Read the article above. What is a pre-nuptial agreement?**

4 **Read the article again and answer true (T) or false (F).**

Example:
Only the rich make pre-nuptial agreements. **F**

1 Bruce asked his girlfriend to marry him.
2 Bruce likes short hair.
3 Suzanne sometimes loses her temper.
4 Suzanne wants Bruce to do the washing up.
5 Bruce wants his wife to get a job.

Grammar focus

5 **Look at the examples below and match them with these meanings.**

a) It isn't necessary but you can do this if you want.
b) It is necessary to do this.
c) Don't do this.

---

have to, don't have to, mustn't (obligation and prohibition)

Obligation:	1	She *has to get* a job.
No obligation:	2	You *don't have to do* much housework.
Prohibition:	3	You *mustn't stay* out late.

Practice

6 **Complete the sentences with the correct form of *have to*, *don't have to* or *mustn't*.**

1 A: Dad, what time <u>do I have to</u> (I) come back home tonight?
  B: You _____ be later than 11 p.m.

2 A: We _____ put some money in the bank. Our account is empty.
  B: OK. And we _____ write any cheques for about a week.

3 A: You _____ use that washing machine. It's dangerous.
  B: OK, but I _____ do some washing soon.

4 A: What time _____ (we) leave?
  B: We've got lots of time. We _____ leave yet.

5 A: I _____ forget to see him. It's important.
  B: I know it's important, but you _____ go and see him. You can phone.

6 A: Be careful. You _____ lose your passport.
  B: It's OK. I _____ have a passport for Spain.

7 **In pairs, practise the dialogues.**

Get talking

8 **Make your own smart agreements.**

1 In pairs, choose one or two of the situations below and discuss how to make them successful.

SITUATIONS
Imagine you are going to:
• marry a millionaire/ess
• go into business with a friend
• travel round the world with a friend
• share a flat with someone you don't know well

---

2 Individually or in pairs, choose one of the situations you discussed and write notes for your own smart agreement.

OUR SMART AGREEMENT
* I have to:

don't have to:

mustn't:

* The other person has to:

doesn't have to:

mustn't:

Language to go

A: We mustn't be late.
B: I know, but we don't have to leave yet. It's too early.

> GRAMMAR REFERENCE PAGE 115
> PRACTICE PAGE 102

Vocabulary Food: meat, vegetables, fruit
Grammar The future with *going to* and *will*
Language to go Planned and spontaneous decisions

Australian barbecue

Vocabulary and speaking

1 **Put the food in the picture in the correct columns.**

Meat	Vegetables	Fruit
beef		

2 **Talk to other students about eating habits where you live.**

1 Do people generally eat a lot of meat?
2 What type of meat do you cook most often?
3 Do you eat a lot of fruit and vegetables?
4 Are there many vegetarians? Is it easy to find vegetarian food in restaurants?
5 Do people generally invite friends to eat at home or in restaurants?
6 Do you often have barbecues? If so, what food do you cook?

onions
beef
lamb
strawberries
carrots

Listening

3 📟 **Listen to Lisa and Mike planning a barbecue, then answer the questions.**

1 Where are they going to have their barbecue?
2 What's the problem?
3 What's the solution?

4 **Listen again and tick (✓) the food words from Exercise 1 as you hear them. Which words do they not mention?**

Grammar focus

5 **Look at the examples below and underline the correct words in these explanations.**

1 We use *will* / *going to* when we have already made the decision.
2 We use *will* / *going to* when we make the decision as we speak.

Decisions for the future	
going to	*will*
(?) What *are* we *going to* cook?	What *will* you make?
(+) We *'re going to* start with salads.	OK then, I *'ll* make vegetable kebabs.
(–) She *isn't going to* cook.	So we *won't* have meat.

oranges

pineapple

green pepper

apples

chicken

mushrooms

pork

Practice

6 For each sentence, choose the correct continuation, a) or b).

Example: 1 – b)   2 – a)

1 I'm not sure what I'm going to do today.
2 I'm afraid I can't meet you this evening.

a) I'm going to visit my mum.
b) Perhaps I'll visit my mum.

3 OK, what shall we eat tonight?
4 I bought some spaghetti this morning.

a) I know! I'll make some pasta.
b) So we're going to have pasta tonight.

5 I've decided what to get for her birthday.
6 I've finished my book and I'm bored.

a) I'll buy you a new book then.
b) I'm going to buy her a book.

7 You can't wear those shorts to the party.
8 What are you going to wear to the party?

a) OK then, I'll wear jeans.
b) I'm going to wear jeans.

Get talking

7 You want to invite a British family to eat with you. In groups, plan the meal.

1 Discuss when and where to have the meal, and what food and drink to have.

2 List your decisions. Then say what food and drink each one of you will make or bring.

   I'll make / bring ...

3 Tell the class what your group plans to do.

   We're going to have the meal on / at ...
   Danny's going to bring / make ...

Language to go

A: I'm going to cook tonight.
B: Right. I'll go to a restaurant then.

> GRAMMAR REFERENCE PAGE 115

> PRACTICE PAGE 102

LESSON **27**
Adjectives

Vocabulary   Medical symptoms; the body
Grammar   Adjectives ending in *-ed* and *-ing*
Language to go   Describing how you feel

Irritating illnesses

Vocabulary and speaking

1   **Match the symptoms with people in the picture.**

Example: a headache – D

> a headache
> a sore throat
> a rash   a cold
> a backache
> a stomachache
> an earache

2   **Listen, check and repeat.**

3   **In pairs, take turns to begin this dialogue. Each time, complete it with a symptom from Exercise 1 and a piece of advice from the list below.**

A: *What's the matter?*
B: *I've got ...*
A: *You should be careful ...*

- Don't carry heavy things.
- Wear a hat and scarf when you go outside.
- Have a hot drink of honey and lemon.
- Sit quietly and try to relax.
- Take lots of Vitamin C.
- Try not to scratch it.
- Don't eat any more of that.

Reading

4   **Read the letters opposite to Doctor Monica about medical problems and answer the questions.**

1   Which symptom(s) from Exercise 1 does each reader have?
2   Which reader is: a) worried?   b) depressed?   c) annoyed?
3   Which picture on page 57 (A–G) shows the cause of each reader's problem?

5   **Read and match the problems (1–3) with the answers (a–c).**

Grammar focus

6   **Look at the examples below and underline the correct words in these explanations.**

1   Adjectives ending in *-ing* / *-ed* describe how you feel.
2   Adjectives ending in *-ing* / *-ed* describe what or who makes you feel this way.

Adjectives ending in *-ed* and *-ing*		
Jez was	*surprised* *annoyed*	because his symptoms were	*surprising.* *annoying.*

56

27

This week: **Irritating Illnesses**

Doctor Monica's helpline

YOUR PROBLEMS

 A B C D E F G

1 Dear Doctor Monica,
Two weeks ago, I was enjoying the beautiful spring flowers in the park when I got a terrible sore throat. At home, I was really surprised to see that my eyes were very red. It isn't a cold, but I still don't feel right. It's really annoying because I love playing sports but I really don't want to go outside at the moment. What's wrong with me?
Alex King, Manchester

2 Dear Doctor Monica,
I used to eat chocolate every day. But a month ago, I started getting terrible headaches. Then I read an interesting article which said that chocolate can cause this. I was completely shocked. Now I don't eat any chocolate and I feel fine ... but it's also a bit depressing. Can I really never eat chocolate again?
Sarah Kahn, New York City

3 Dear Doctor Monica,
My family has two dogs and a cat. I'm at university now and, when I come home for the holidays, I get a rash on my neck and my eyes are really red and sore. It's a bit embarrassing – everyone thinks I'm crying! I'm really worried because my parents think we should find another home for the animals. I don't want them to go. Is it necessary?
Frances May, London

DOCTOR MONICA WRITES BACK

a You are not with your animals all the time, so perhaps it won't be necessary for them to live somewhere else. When you are home, try not to touch the dogs or cat too often. They should be given regular baths and, of course, they should never sleep on your bed.

b It sounds as if you have hay fever and are allergic to the pollen from trees and plants. You are doing the right thing. Stay inside and keep the windows shut. Don't be too worried – you'll be OK when the spring is over.

c Food allergies can be very frightening because the cause is often difficult to find. You know the cause of your problem, so you'll be fine now. But you shouldn't eat chocolate again. I'm sorry!

Practice

7 **Underline** the correct adjectives in the dialogues.

Example:
A: I'm really *surprised* / *surprising*. This is such a terrible cold.
B: It's not *surprised* / *surprising*. You never wear the right clothes.

1 A: That rash is really *worried* / *worrying*.
  B: The doctor isn't very *worried* / *worrying*.

2 A: I've just read an *interested* / *interesting* article on allergies. It says lots of them are caused by pollution.
  B: I know. It's a shame more politicians aren't *interested* / *interesting* in the problem.

3 A: I was *shocked* / *shocking* to hear he's in hospital.
  B: And nobody in the family has been to visit. It's quite *shocked* / *shocking*.

4 A: He used to be *frightened* / *frightening* of doctors.
  B: Well, he's not *frightened* / *frightening* any more. He is a doctor.

8 **In pairs, practise the dialogues.**

Get talking

9 **Roleplay a visit to the doctor.**

Group A: Turn to page 84.
Group B: Turn to page 87.

Language to go

A: Oh dear. Life is really depressing.
B: Of course you're depressed. I'm very expensive.

> GRAMMAR REFERENCE PAGE 115
> PRACTICE PAGE 103

57

Vocabulary Furniture and fittings
Grammar Present perfect to describe present result
Language to go Talking about changes you can see

Changing rooms

Vocabulary

1 Match the words with furniture and fittings in the photos below.

Example: sofa – H̶

1 armchair	7 curtains
2 bookshelf	8 light
3 cushion	9 fireplace
4 carpet	10 sink
5 cooker	11 rug
6 cupboard	12 washing machine

2 Match the sentences with the responses.

Example: **1– e)**

1 I don't like the table that colour.
2 We need a bookshelf.
3 The corner cupboard doesn't look very good.
4 I hate the floor in this room.
5 Those old cushions on the armchairs are really ugly.

a) We can make one.
b) Let's re-cover them and put them on the sofa.
c) Why don't we change the carpet or polish the floorboards?
d) Let's move it to the other side of the room or remove it completely.
e) Shall we paint it blue, then?

TV Choice

This week, two pairs of neighbours, Michelle and Jason Cole and Megan and Peter Smythe, work with 'Changing Rooms' interior designers to change a room in each other's home. They have two days and can each spend a maximum of £500. To see the results, watch 'Changing Rooms' on Tuesday evening.

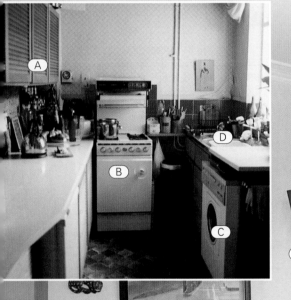

Reading and listening

3 Read about the programme 'Changing Rooms' in TV Choice and answer the questions.

1 What is Michelle and Jason Cole's relationship with Megan and Peter Smythe?
2 What are they going to do?
3 How long do they have to do it?
4 How much can they spend?

4 ▭▭ Listen to Michelle and Jason when they see their new room.

1 Are they generally positive or negative about the changes?
2 Who likes it more, Michelle or Jason?

5 Listen again. Match the columns to describe what their neighbours have done.

Example: *1– e)*

1 They've removed   a) the sofa.
2 They've painted   b) the armchairs.
3 They've made   c) the walls bright red.
4 They've moved   d) new curtains.
5 They've re-covered   e) the carpet.
6 They've put   f) the books in the cupboard.

Grammar focus

6 Look at the examples below and <u>underline</u> the correct words in these explanations.

1 We use the present perfect to talk about a *present / past* action.
2 We *can / can't* see the result in the present.

Present perfect	
Present result	**Past action**
What a change!	(?) What *have* they *done*?
Look at the floor.	(+) They *'ve polished* the floorboards.
Are they new armchairs?	(–) No, she *hasn't bought* new armchairs.

Practice

7 Look at the photo of Megan and Peter's new kitchen below. Use the words in the box to describe the changes their neighbours have made to their old kitchen (on page 58).

Example: *They've put the washing machine in a cupboard.*

the washing machine   the walls   the sink
the floor   the cooker   cupboards

Get talking ...

8 In pairs, find the six differences that the 'Changing Rooms' team has made to another room.

Student A: Turn to pages 84 and 85.
Student B: Turn to page 88.

... and writing

9 Write a paragraph for a letter to a friend.

1 Describe recent changes you have made either in your home or in your life.
2 What are the results of these changes?

Language to go

A: Have you decorated the house?
B: We've painted the walls but we haven't done anything else.

> GRAMMAR REFERENCE PAGE 115
> PRACTICE PAGE 103

Vocabulary	Table manners
Function	Permission
Language to go	Asking for, giving and refusing permission

How rude!

2   ❝ It's impolite to put your elbows on a table at mealtimes. ❞

1   ❝ It's only OK to kiss in public in the evening when it's dark. ❞

Vocabulary

1 Look at the picture and answer the questions.

Example: Who is snapping his / her fingers? **C**

1 Who has got his / her elbows on the table?
2 Who is kissing someone in public?
3 Who is pointing at someone?
4 Who is eating with his / her fingers?
5 Who is blowing his / her nose?

Reading and speaking

2 In pairs, decide which sentences, 1–10, are true (T) or false (F):

a) in your country   b) in the UK

Listening

3 **Listen and match the conversations with situations described in sentences 1–10.**

Example: A – **6**

10   ❝ When you meet a person for the first time, it's polite to kiss him / her once on the left cheek. ❞

9   ❝ When you go to a dinner party, it's polite to take some food, perhaps some ice cream or a cake. ❞

Language focus

4 Look at the examples below and match these headings with the columns a), b) and c).

• Refusing permission   • Asking for permission   • Giving permission

a) _____	b) _____	c) _____
1 *May we smoke* in here?	*Yes, certainly.*	*I'm sorry, but* it's a no-smoking area.
2 *Can I borrow* your pen, please?		*I'm sorry. I need it* myself.
3 *Could I have* a glass of water?	*Yes, of course.*	
4 *Is it OK if I sit* here?	*Yes, sure.*	*No, sorry.* This seat is taken.

5 **Listen to questions 1–4 above. You will hear each question twice. Which sounds more polite, a) or b)?**

Example: 1 – **b)**

6 **Listen and repeat the polite questions and responses.**

3 66 In a restaurant, it's rude to snap your fingers when you want a waiter or waitress. 99

4 66 When someone invites you to a restaurant for a meal, it's rude to offer to pay for your meal. 99

5 66 When people invite you to their house for dinner, it's impolite to be very late. 99

6 66 When you are at a friend's house, it's OK to make a phone call without asking your friend. 99

7 66 When you want to smoke in a public place or in someone's house, it's polite to ask for permission. 99

8 66 It's very rude to eat when you are walking down a street. 99

Practice

7 **Use the prompts to make sentences asking for, giving and refusing permission.**

Example: could / use your pencil?
A: *Could I use your pencil, please?*
B: *Yes, of course.* (✔)

		Response
1	may / give you some advice?	(✔)
2	OK / take this chair?	(✗)
3	can / have an apple?	(✔)
4	OK / smoke?	(✗)
5	could / borrow your book?	(✗)
6	may / leave my bag here?	(✔)

8 **In pairs, take turns to ask for permission and respond, using the prompts above.**

Get talking ...

9 **In pairs, make and respond to requests.**

Student A: Turn to page 85.
Student B: Turn to page 88.

... and writing

10 **Make and respond to written requests.**

1 Write two short notes, one to your teacher and one to your partner, asking for permission to do something. Give your notes to them.

2 Write a response to the note you receive.

> GRAMMAR REFERENCE PAGE 115

> PRACTICE PAGE 104

Vocabulary   Verbs and their opposites
Grammar   *Would* + infinitive (without *to*)
Language to go   Talking about imaginary situations

What would you do for love?

Vocabulary

1   <u>Underline</u> the correct words.

Example: I was really pleased that he
remembered / *forgot* our anniversary.

1   Jim and Sandra got *married* / *divorced* last
    week. It was a lovely wedding.
2   I want to *buy* / *sell* my car. I need the money.
3   Richard *refused* / *agreed* to lend me his
    computer. He's bringing it now.
4   Did you *lose* / *find* your wallet yesterday? Is
    that it, under the sofa?
5   Don't *lie* / *tell the truth*. I know you took my
    money!
6   We love it here, so we don't want to *move* /
    stay.

Reading

2   **Read and match the stories below with the
    pictures on the right.**

3   **Read again and answer true (T) or false (F).**

Example: The dangerous pedestrian caused eight
car accidents. *T*

1   The dangerous pedestrian wanted a boyfriend.
2   David Hillman would send her to prison.
3   John Mason sold his things to buy his
    girlfriend a car.
4   Chris Drew would do the same for his
    girlfriend.
5   The jealous wife sold her husband's clothes
    for $5.
6   Her husband had another woman.
7   In the same situation, Monica Jenkins would
    do the same thing.

Would YOU do that for love?

Dangerous pedestrian

A WOMAN IN MOSCOW went to prison because she caused eight car accidents. Every time she saw a good-looking man driving a car, she walked in front of the car. She thought the men would feel badly about hitting her and so they would ask her out on a date.

I'm not sure what I would do with someone like this, but I wouldn't feel sorry for her.
Sara Davies from Brighton

I wouldn't put this woman in prison. I'd get her some psychiatric help.
David Hillman from Edinburgh

True love or true madness?

A MAN SOLD everything he had to buy his girlfriend a ring. John Mason sold his car, his guitar, his stereo and even some of his clothes. Then he borrowed another £5,000. The ring his girlfriend liked was £15,000.

Nice guy, but what an idiot! I would never do that. My girlfriend would think I was crazy.
Chris Drew from Cardiff

Where is this man? I'd marry him tomorrow. I hope his girlfriend knows how lucky she is.
Cynthia Farey from Liverpool

Jealous wife

SHEILA PORTER sold her husband's Porsche sports car because she saw him with another woman. The car was parked outside their house and Sheila put a sign in the window: 'For Sale - $5'. Someone bought it immediately.

In simple English, I'd kill her.
Paul Jones from London

I can certainly understand this woman. I would do the same in her situation.
Monica Jenkins from Exeter

Grammar focus

4 **Look at the examples below and choose a) or b) to complete the explanation.**

We use *would* + infinitive (without *to*) for:
a) something we plan to do in the future.
b) something we are imagining.

---

would + infinitive (without *to*)

(+) I*'d* (I *would*) *marry* him tomorrow.
(−) I *wouldn't put* her in prison.
(?) *Would* you *do* that for love?
   Yes, I *would*. / No, I *wouldn't*.

---

5 Listen and repeat. Pay attention to contracted forms.

Practice

6 **Complete these dialogues about imaginary situations with *would* or *wouldn't* and the verbs in the box, where necessary.**

> lend   move   marry   sell (x3)   stay   buy (x2)

Example:
A: Your friend wants to borrow a lot of money. <u>Would</u> you <u>lend</u> him some?
B: Yes, I think I <u>would</u>.

1 A: OK. You really need some money, quickly. What _____ you _____ ?
   B: Well, I _____ certainly _____ the television, but I _____ the stereo. I like music too much.

2 A: You win a lot of money. _____ you _____ a really expensive car?
   B: No, I _____ , but I _____ a boat. I love sailing.

3 A: OK. You can live in any country in the world. Where _____ you _____ to?
   B: I _____ right here, with you.

4 A: You've only known your boyfriend / girlfriend for two months but you are very much in love. _____ you _____ him / her?
   B: No, I _____ .

7 **In pairs, practise the dialogues but say what <u>you</u> would do.**

Get talking

8 **Create a 'What would you do?' questionnaire.**

Pair A: Turn to page 85.
Pair B: Turn to page 89.

Language to go

A: Would you marry for money?
B: No, I wouldn't. I'd only marry for love.

> GRAMMAR REFERENCE PAGE 116
> PRACTICE PAGE 104

LESSON **31**
The past

Vocabulary Crime: word building
Grammar Past simple passive
Language to go Describing a crime

The art of crime

Vocabulary and speaking

1 **Complete the table.**

Crime	Criminal	Verb	Meaning
bank robbery	bank robber	to rob a bank	to take illegally (and often violently) from a bank
	murderer		to kill
burglary		to burgle	to take illegally from a building, especially a house
	mugger	to mug	to attack and take something from a person
shoplifting			to take from a shop without paying
car theft		to steal a car	to take a car illegally

2 **In pairs, put the crimes in order of seriousness (1 = the most serious, 6 = the least serious).**

3 **In pairs, decide what should happen to each type of criminal. Should they:**

a) go to prison? (say for how long)
b) pay a fine? (say how much)
c) be executed?

Example: *A murderer should go to prison for 30 years.*

Listening

4 **Look at this painting and answer the questions.**

1 It's called the *Mona Lisa* in English. Do you know what it's called in your language?
2 Who painted it?
3 Where can you see it today?

5 In 1911, the *Mona Lisa* disappeared. Listen to the story and match the questions with the answers.

1 Who had the idea for the theft?
2 Who stole the painting?
3 Who believed the copies were real?

a) Eduardo de Valfierno
b) rich collectors
c) Vincenzo Perugia

6 **Listen again and answer true (T) or false (F).**

Example:
The *Mona Lisa* was painted by Michelangelo. **F**

1 The painting was never found.
2 The thief was arrested.
3 Six copies of the painting were made.
4 Perugia was paid 500,000 lire for his help.

Grammar focus

7 **Look at the examples below and <u>underline</u> the correct word in the explanation.**

We use the *passive / active* when we are more interested in the action than in the person or thing that did the action.

Active sentences			Passive sentences		
Subject	Verb	Object	Subject	Verb	(Agent)
Da Vinci	painted	the *Mona Lisa*.	It	*was painted*	by da Vinci.
Someone	stole	the painting.	The painting	*was stolen*.	

Passive questions			
Question word	Auxiliary	Subject	Past participle
Who	*was*	the *Mona Lisa*	*painted by*?
When	*was*	the painting	*stolen*?

Practice

8 **<u>Underline</u> the correct form of the verb.**

Example: I *mugged* / <u>*was mugged*</u> in the street yesterday.

1 They *robbed* / *were robbed* the bank of £50,000.
2 Our house *burgled* / *was burgled* last month.
3 The police *arrested* / *was arrested* the man for shoplifting.
4 The woman *murdered* / *was murdered* the man.
5 My car *stole* / *was stolen* yesterday.
6 They *executed* / *were executed* the murderer.
7 The bank manager *murdered* / *was murdered* by the robber.
8 They *found* / *were found* the videos in the shoplifter's bag.
9 The mugger *took* / *was taken* my wallet.
10 The thief *paid* / *was paid* £50,000 for stealing the painting.

Get talking

9 **In pairs, ask and answer about a famous crime.**

Student A: Turn to page 86.
Student B: Turn to page 89.

Student A: Turn to page 86.
Student B: Turn to page 89.

Language to go

A: When was your car stolen?
B: Last year. The thieves were never found.

> GRAMMAR REFERENCE PAGE 116
> PRACTICE PAGE 105

Vocabulary   Phrasal verbs
Grammar   Verbs with *-ing* form / infinitive (with *to*)
Language to go   Talking about changing habits

Willpower

Can you say no?

Can you do things you want to do even if they're difficult? Can you finish what you start?

Read each situation and choose a), b) or c). Then check the key on page 86.

1   *You have stopped eating sweets but you want something to eat. There's a box of chocolates in the cupboard. Do you decide to:*

a) eat all the chocolates but not buy any more?
b) <u>throw away</u> the whole box?
c) eat one or two and then throw away the rest?

2   *You realise you always contact a particular friend before he / she contacts you. Do you decide to:*

a) phone anyway and say nothing about it?
b) wait for your friend to phone you?
c) phone and say what you think?

3   *You realise smoking is ruining your health. Do you decide to:*

a) <u>give up</u> smoking next week and open a new packet?
b) give up smoking completely and chew some chewing gum?
c) <u>cut down</u> and only smoke one or two this evening?

4   *You don't enjoy doing exercise but you are getting fat. You <u>take up</u> jogging. As soon as you start, you meet a good friend who invites you for coffee. Do you decide to:*

a) stop and have a cup of coffee with your friend?
b) say you don't need to have a cup of coffee and <u>carry on</u> jogging?
c) say you'll meet him / her in five minutes and only jog round the park once?

Reading

1   Do the questionnaire to find out how much willpower you have.

Vocabulary

2   Find phrasal verbs <u>underlined</u> in the questionnaire that mean the following.

Example: begin – *take up*

1   continue
2   stop
3   do less
4   put in the rubbish bin

Grammar focus

3   Look at the examples below. Then say if these verbs are followed by an *-ing* form or an infinitive form (with *to*).

take up   promise   learn   cut down

Verbs with *-ing* form / infinitive (with *to*)	
-ing form	Infinitive (with *to*)
(?) Do you *give up smoking*?	Do you *decide to phone*?
(+) You *carry on jogging*.	You *want to eat* something.
(–) You *don't enjoy doing* exercise.	You *don't need to have* a cup of coffee.

Practice

4 Complete the paragraph with the correct form of the verbs in brackets.

I was going to Spain on holiday so I decided <u>to take up</u> (take up) Spanish. I wanted
(1) _____ (have) time to study properly so I cut down on my hours at work. However, I gave up (2) _____ (go) to classes a month before the holiday. I couldn't carry on (3) _____ (have) lessons in the evenings because I was too busy. I didn't enjoy (4) _____ (listen) to my Spanish cassettes very much, so I gave that up too. I didn't want (5) _____ (carry) a heavy suitcase on the journey, so I decided
(6) _____ (throw away) my big grammar book and buy a little phrasebook instead. But when I arrived in Spain, I didn't need
(7) _____ (speak) Spanish at all. Everyone spoke English!

Get talking

5 In groups, play the Willpower Game.

1 Take turns to throw a coin. If you throw 'heads', go forward one square. If you throw 'tails', go forward two squares.

2 When you land on a square, talk about the topic. Tell the truth about yourself. (Move back one square if your sentence is incorrect.)

   Example: *I've never smoked.*
   I used to smoke but I gave up smoking three years ago.
   I haven't given up yet, but I've cut down.
   I need to give up smoking.

3 The winner is the first player to reach the end.

Language to go

A: Have you got a cigarette?
B: Didn't you decide to give up?
A: No. I only gave up buying cigarettes.

> GRAMMAR REFERENCE PAGE 116
> PRACTICE PAGE 105

Vocabulary	Regular activities: verb + noun combinations
Grammar	Subject and non-subject questions in the present simple
Language to go	Asking questions

A typical day

Vocabulary

1 **Match the columns to find the verbs and nouns that go together.**

Example: *1 – d)*

1 I want to *spend*   a) 100 new *people* every year.
2 I haven't *paid*   b) *a phone call* before we go.
3 We must *empty*   c) *the telephone bill* this month.
4 I need to *make*   d) more *time* with my family.
5 We *employ*   e) *the rubbish* today.

2 **Complete the sentences with verbs from Exercise 1.**

1 I can't _____ this bill. I haven't got enough money.
2 I _____ the rubbish yesterday and it's full again.
3 Last week I _____ a lot of time helping Harry paint his house.
4 Last month we _____ ten new shop assistants.
5 Look at this phone bill! Did you _____ all these phone calls?

Listening

3 🔲 **Listen and find Ron in the picture. What's his job?**

4 **Listen again and answer the questions.**

1 What does Ron do at the parties?   3 Who drives Ron to the parties?
2 What does his wife do to help?   4 Does his wife get jealous?

5 **In groups, talk about one of the following:**

a) an unusual party you have been to   b) the last party you went to

Grammar focus

6 **Look at the examples below and complete these explanations with *subject* or *object*.**

1 In question a), *who* refers to the _____ of the sentence.
2 In question b), *who* refers to the _____ of the sentence.
3 In _____ questions, we don't use the auxiliary *do / does*.

Subject and non-subject questions in the present simple		
Subject	**Verb**	**Object**
The <u>agency</u>	pays	<u>Ron.</u>
a) (Who) *pays* Ron?		b) (Who) *does* the agency *pay*?
The agency.		Ron.

Practice

7 **Complete the questions using the prompts in brackets.**

1 A: <u>Who gets up</u> (who / get up) first in your house?
   B: Usually I do.
   A: And _____ (what time / you / get up)?
   B: About 7.30.

2 A: _____ (you / have) a computer at home?
   B: Yes.
   A: _____ (who / use) it the most?
   B: My younger brother.

3 A: _____ (who / make) the most phone calls?
   B: I do, I think.
   A: _____ (who / you phone) the most?
   B: My friend Judith.

4 A: _____ (who / pay) the bills in your house?
   B: My mother and father both pay.

5 A: _____ (who usually / do) the cooking?
   B: I don't, that's for sure.
   A: And _____ (who / empty) the rubbish?
   B: Nobody. Look at the mess.

6 A: _____ (who / you spend) more time with, your friends or your family?
   B: My friends.
   A: _____ (how many evenings a week / you stay) at home?
   B: Four or five.
   A: _____ (who / spend) the most time in the house?
   B: My mother, I suppose.

8  **Listen and check your answers.**

Get talking

9 **In pairs, ask and answer about your home routines.**

1 Take turns to ask and answer the questions in Exercise 7.

2 What are the similarities and differences in your home routines?

Language to go

A: Who uses the phone most in your house?
B: My daughter.
A: Who does she phone?
B: Everyone.

> GRAMMAR REFERENCE PAGE 116
> PRACTICE PAGE 106

Vocabulary   Technical equipment
Grammar   Relative clauses with *which, that, who* and *where*
Language to go   Describing people, places and things

How things work

Vocabulary and speaking

1 **Look at the names of technical equipment and answer the questions below.**

screen

keyboard

remote control

Example:
Which two have a screen and a keyboard?
a), f)

a) computer
b) digital camera
c) mobile phone
d) photocopier
e) printer
f) laptop
g) scanner
h) digital TV

1 Which two can put pictures or text on paper?
2 Which two make pictures that you can look at on a computer?
3 Which one has a screen and a remote control?
4 Which one can go in your pocket and rings when someone wants to speak to you?

2 🎧 **Listen and check.**

3 🎧 **Listen and repeat. Pay attention to stress.**

4 **Discuss answers to these questions.**

1 Which of the technical equipment in Exercise 1 have you got?
2 Which would you like to have?
3 Which do you think is the most useful?

Reading

5 **Read about digital TV and answer true (T) or false (F).**

Example: We can communicate with digital TVs. *T*

1 You can't send e-mails from digital TVs.
2 Traditional TV pictures take more space than digital pictures.
3 Digital pictures of buildings are sent many times.
4 Moving pictures take more space than still pictures.
5 You can only receive digital TV on a special TV.

Grammar focus

6 **Look at the examples below and complete these explanations.**

To introduce relative clauses we use:
1 _____ for places.
2 _____ or _____ for things.
3 _____ or _____ for people.

Relative clauses with *which, that, who* and *where*		
They send a lot of pictures of people	*who* / *that*	are walking.
They only send the parts of the picture	*which* / *that*	change.
A studio is a place *where* they make programmes.		

Practice

7 **Make complete sentences with *who, which, that* or *where*.**

Example: *1 – c)* A mechanic is someone *who / that* mends cars.

1 A mechanic is someone
2 A garage is a place
3 A brake is something
4 A cook is someone
5 A cooker is a machine
6 A cash machine is a place
7 A credit card is something
8 A photographer is a person

a) makes meals.
b) takes pictures.
c) mends cars.
d) makes food hot.
e) is used to pay for things.
f) stops a car or a bike.
g) they mend cars.
h) you can get money when banks are closed.

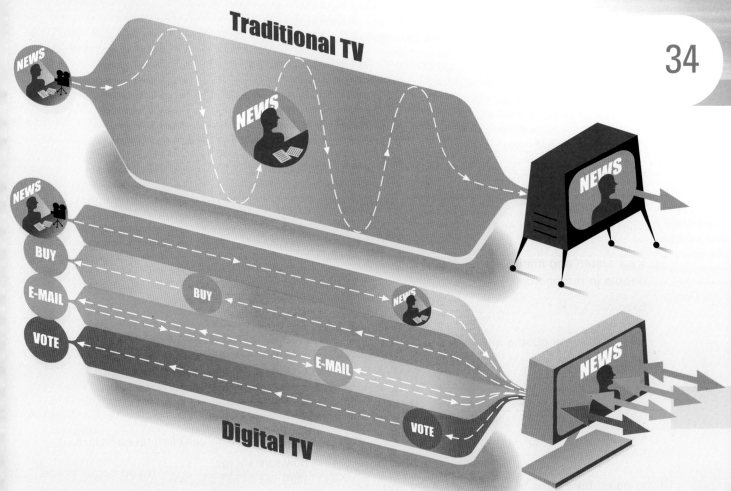

Traditional TV

Digital TV

34

What is digital TV?

In the past, we usually just sat and watched TV. But digital TV is something that we can communicate with. We can easily buy direct from advertisements or answer quiz questions. We can also send and receive e-mails and vote. And it will be possible for us all to watch any programme, when we want, without a video.

How does digital TV work?

As we know, a TV studio is a place where they make programmes. Pictures are sent from the TV studio to our homes. Traditional TV uses a lot of space to send the pictures. On digital TV systems pictures don't use much space so this system can send and receive more information.

How do they make the TV programme smaller?

Digital TV systems only send the parts of the picture that change. So they send a picture of a building once, because it doesn't move. But they send a lot of pictures of people who are walking or cars which are moving.

How does the TV picture arrive on my TV?

You need a special TV, or a special box for your non-digital TV, which can put the pictures together. Then you can watch your favourite TV programme!

Get writing and talking

8 **In groups, play the Definitions Game.**

1 Individually, write definitions of six people, places or things.

Example: *A person who flies planes.*
A thing which plays CDs.

2 In groups, take turns to read out your definitions and guess the answers.

> GRAMMAR REFERENCE PAGE 116

> PRACTICE PAGE 106

Language to go

A: I want a camera that's easy to use.
B: I know a place where you can buy a really good one.

Vocabulary   Sounds people make
Grammar   Present deduction with *must be, might be, can't be*
Language to go   Making deductions

What's that noise?

Vocabulary and speaking

1   📼 **Listen and match the sounds with people in the photos.**

Example: 1 – H

2   **Now match the people in the photos with these verbs.**

Example: A – yawn

| shout   cry   whistle   scream |
| cheer   yawn   clap   laugh |

3   **In pairs, take turns to make the noises and say what your partner is doing.**

Example: You're yawning.

Listening

4   📼 **Listen to this radio phone-in competition and answer true (T) or false (F).**

1   Marion and Steve have to guess what the people's jobs are.
2   The prize is four tickets to a football match.
3   They both win a prize.

5   **Listen again and answer the questions.**

1   Which possible places and jobs does Marion mention?
2   What is Marion's final answer?
3   Which four possible jobs does Steve mention?
4   What is Steve's final answer?
5   What is the correct answer?

6   **In pairs, make a list of the sounds that Marion and Steve heard. How many can you remember?**

Example: people talking

Grammar focus

7   **Look at the examples below and match them with their meanings.**

Example: 1 – d)

a) It's possible that he's a bus driver.
b) It's my opinion that he isn't a taxi driver.
c) It's a fact that he isn't a taxi driver.
d) It's a fact that he's a bus driver.
e) It's my opinion that he's a bus driver.

---

must be, might be, can't be (present deduction)

How sure are you?
100% yes   1   He's a bus driver.
                    2   He *must be* a bus driver.
        50%   3   He *might be* a bus driver.
                    4   He *can't be* a taxi driver.
100% no   5   He isn't a taxi driver.

72

35

Practice

8 Complete the sentences with *must be*, *might be* or *can't be*.

Example:

A: What's that noise upstairs?

B: I don't know, but it _can't be_ the cat. I saw it go outside a minute ago.

1 A: Who's that kissing Gillian?

  B: She got married last Saturday so it _____ her husband.

2 A: I can't find my glasses.

  B: They _____ in the bathroom. You sometimes leave them there.

3 A: How long was your journey?

  B: Twenty-six hours.

  A: You _____ really tired.

4 A: Sam never does any work for his exams but he always passes.

  B: Well, they _____ very difficult exams then.

5 A: Listen to his accent. He _____ American.

  B: Not necessarily. He _____ from Canada.

6 A: I'm hungry.

  B: You _____ hungry. You've just eaten a three-course meal.

7 A: Linda and Jeff are going on holiday to Bermuda again. That's their fourth holiday there this year.

  B: They _____ quite rich then.

8 A: I can't find the scissors.

  B: I had them a minute ago, so they _____ far away.

Get talking

9 📼 **Take part in the radio phone-in competition from Exercise 4. What is this person's job?**

1 Listen to the first clue. In pairs, list all the possible jobs for the sounds you hear. Tell the class.

2 Listen to the next clue. Are all the jobs still possible? If not, be ready to explain why. Tell the class.

3 Listen to the last clue. You should only have one possible job. Tell the class.

4 Listen to the complete sequence. What is the job? Were you correct?

10 📼 **Now listen to the next sequence of sounds and follow the same instructions.**

Language to go

A: That might be John at the door.

B: No, it can't be. He's in the USA.

A: Then it must be Pete.

> GRAMMAR REFERENCE PAGE 116

> PRACTICE PAGE 107

LESSON 36
The future

Vocabulary   Time expressions with *in, on, at* or no preposition
Grammar   Present continuous for future time
Language to go   Talking about future arrangements

A football fan's website

Vocabulary

1 Put these time expressions in the correct columns.

- night
- tomorrow morning
- 10 a.m.
- the morning
- this Thursday
- next Monday evening
- last Friday afternoon
- the evening
- 6.45 p.m.
- last night
- Monday afternoon
- the afternoon
- Thursday
- yesterday morning
- midnight
- midday
- this evening

in	*on*	*at*	no preposition
		night	

2 Complete the sentences with a preposition where necessary.

Example: I don't sleep very well **at** night.

1 Kim came home _____ 4 a.m. yesterday.
2 Where did you go _____ last night?
3 I'm going to a football match _____ Saturday afternoon.
4 I'll phone you _____ the afternoon.
5 We're having a dinner party _____ Friday evening.
6 Her plane left _____ midnight.
7 Did you see Anne _____ yesterday evening?
8 I have to go to the dentist _____ this afternoon.

Reading and listening

3 Read the webpage of a Manchester United football fan and answer the questions.

1 Which three countries are they travelling to?
2 How many matches are they going to?
3 How long is their trip?

4  Listen to a phone conversation between Peter and another fan. Change the information on the webpage.

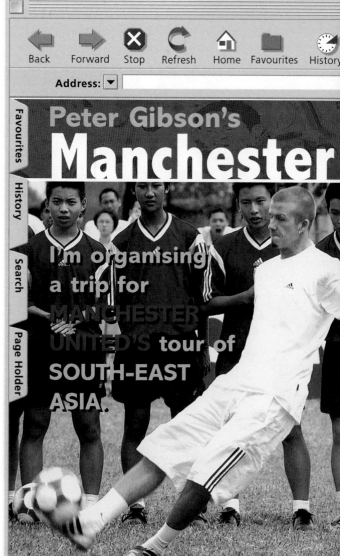

Back   Forward   Stop   Refresh   Home   Favourites   History

Address: ▼

Favourites
History
Search
Page Holder

Peter Gibson's
Manchester

I'm organising a trip for MANCHESTER UNITED'S tour of SOUTH-EAST ASIA.

36

Grammar focus

5 Look at the examples below and <u>underline</u> the correct words in these explanations.

1 We use the present continuous to talk about *a possible future event* / *a definite future arrangement*.

2 When we use the present continuous for the future, we usually *need to* / *don't need to* say the time.

Present continuous for future time
(+) We *'re leaving* on Monday morning.
(−) On Thursday we *'re not having* lunch at Raffles.
(?) What time *are* we *arriving* in Kuala Lumpur?

Practice

6 Use the information from Exercise 4 to write five sentences about the trip.

Example: *They aren't leaving Heathrow at 12 p.m.; they're leaving at 10 p.m.*

Get talking ...

7 Arrange a game of football with friends.

1 Look at your diary page for next week. Choose a day you would like to play a game of football with your friends. Write this in your diary.

2 Think of six other activities you're doing next week and add these and times to your diary.

3 You already have seven people for your team. You have to find four more people who are free at the time you're having the football match.

4 The winner is the first to get four people to complete his / her team.

... and writing

8 Write and exchange notes to arrange a football match.

1 Write a note to a friend and ask him / her to play football with you. Give the date and time.

2 Give your note to another student.

3 Write a reply to the note you received. Check your diary and, if you can't play at that time, explain why you can't.

Language to go

A: Are you playing football next Saturday?
B: No. I can't. I'm studying for my exams.

> GRAMMAR REFERENCE PAGE 117
> PRACTICE PAGE 107

Vocabulary   Adjectives and their opposites
Grammar   *So* + adjective / *such* + noun
Language to go   Emphasising feelings and opinions

It was so funny!

Vocabulary

1   **Put the adjectives in the box in the correct columns.**

> ugly   mean   delicious   attractive   terrible   special   full   great
> hungry   generous   serious   disgusting   funny   ordinary

	adjective	opposite
Example: Something good to eat is:	delicious	disgusting

1   Someone who's had enough to eat is:
2   Someone/thing that you like very much is:
3   Someone/thing that is amusing is:
4   Someone/thing that is good-looking is:
5   Someone/thing that is usual or common is:
6   Someone who doesn't like spending
money is:

2   **Underline the correct words in the letter.**

Dear Elisa,
I must tell you the news. I finally asked Miranda to go out with me – you know, that **attractive** / **ugly** woman from the office. As it was a
(1) **special** / **ordinary** occasion, I booked the best theatre tickets possible and Miranda wore a new dress. It was a comedy, 'Laugh a Minute', and we certainly did that. It was really
(2) **serious** / **funny**. Afterwards we went to my favourite restaurant and as usual the food was
(3) **delicious** / **disgusting**. I was particularly
(4) **full** / **hungry** – no lunch – so I ate lots.
The trouble was, it was a bit expensive and I didn't have enough money for the bill.
But Miranda is very (5) **generous** / **mean** and she paid. When we left the restaurant it was raining. There was no money left for a taxi so we had to walk home. Miranda seemed a bit upset. I don't know why. I thought it was a
(6) **great** / **terrible** evening.
I'll let you know how things continue.
Love,
Tony

Reading

3   **Read the cartoon. What's the joke? Do you think it's funny?**

4   **Read the cartoon again and underline the correct words.**

Example:
Glenda and Jim had a *good* / *bad* day at work.

1   Eating out is a *special* / *ordinary* occasion for them.
2   They are very *tired* / *relaxed*.
3   They have a really *interesting* / *boring* evening.

5   ▭ **Listen to the cartoon conversation and underline *so*, *such* and other stressed words.**

6   **In pairs, read the conversation aloud. Pay attention to stress and intonation.**

37

Grammar focus

7 **Look at the examples below. Is this explanation true (T) or false (F)?**

So and *such* make the words after them stronger.

so + adjective		such (+ adjective) + noun		
I'm *so*	tired.	That was	*such*	a disaster.
	hungry.	I work with		boring people.

Practice

8 **Complete the sentences with *so* or *such*.**

Example: They are <u>such</u> generous people. They often invite friends to restaurants.

1 He didn't laugh at all. He's _____ serious.
2 We didn't have any dinner because we had _____ an enormous lunch.
3 You should have more confidence. You are _____ an attractive person.
4 We fell asleep in the middle of the film. It was _____ boring.
5 Why are you _____ angry? It was an accident.
6 I only agreed to marry him because he cooked _____ a delicious meal.
7 I know I forgot to phone. But what's _____ terrible about that?

Get talking

9 **Talk about some special experiences.**

1 In pairs, tell your partner about three or more of the following. Why was each experience so special?

Example: **The meal was great because it was in such a pretty restaurant and the waiters were so friendly ...**

- a delicious meal you've had lately
- a great place you've visited
- a famous person you've met and who you think is very attractive
- a generous person you've known
- the funniest film / TV programme you've seen recently

2 Tell the class about your partner's most interesting experience and how he / she felt about it.

> GRAMMAR REFERENCE PAGE 117
> PRACTICE PAGE 108

Language to go

A: This evening has gone so fast.
B: Yes, we had such a good time.

LESSON **38**
Present perfect

Vocabulary Immigration
Grammar Present perfect with *for* / *since*
Language to go Talking about how long you have done things

Green card

Vocabulary

1 **Complete the text with words from the box.**

> work permit   green card
> tourist visa   driving licence
> residence permit
> ID (identification) card
> immigration

Going to the USA

Before you visit the USA, check if you need a <u>tourist visa</u> in your passport. Some nationalities need to have one, but others don't. If you want to stay longer than 90 days, you can apply to the (1) _____ department. It is also useful to carry an (2) _____ or a (3) _____ with you so you can prove who you are. If you want to work in the USA, you need a (4) _____ . You also need a (5) _____ so you can live there. When you have these permits, you get a (6) _____ which proves that you have permission to live and work in the USA.

Case number:	247 – Kate Bolton (English), Rod Bolton (American)
Reason for interview:	Kate Bolton – application for green card. Check the marriage is a real marriage.

SUMMARY OF WHAT ROD BOLTON SAID AT THE INTERVIEW

- Kate came to the USA eight months ago but at first she was in San Francisco.
- He (Rod Bolton) met Kate at a party in New York six months ago and they fell in love immediately.
- They were married three months ago.
- Kate is a dance teacher.
- They usually do everything together. They like the same things.

38

Reading and listening

2 Read the notes on page 78 about Kate and Rod Bolton. Why is the immigration officer interviewing them?

3 Read the notes again and complete the table with Rod's information.

	Rod	Kate
Example: When did Kate come to the USA?	8 months ago	

1 Where did she live before she came to New York?
2 When did Kate meet Rod?
3 Where did they meet?
4 When did they get married?
5 What's Kate's job?
6 Do they like doing the same things?

4 📼 Listen to the interview with Kate. Complete the table above with Kate's information. What information is different?

Grammar focus

5 Look at the examples below and answer these questions.

1 When did Kate first meet Rod?
2 When was she last in the UK?
3 Does she live in New York now?

Present perfect with *for* and *since*

(+) I *'ve known* Rod | *for** eight months. / *since** December.

(–) She *hasn't been* to the UK | *for* eight months. / *since* September.

(?) *Has* she *lived* in New York *for* a long time?
   Yes, she *has*.

* We use *for* when we talk about a period of time.
  We use *since* when we talk about a point in time.

Practice

6 Put the expressions in the correct columns.

---
ages May two years nine months 4 a.m.
last summer Friday a couple of days 2001
---

for	*since*
ages	May

7 Complete the dialogue between Rob and the investigator with the correct form of the verbs in brackets. Use *for* or *since*.

I: Nice cat. <u>Have you had</u> (you have) him <u>for</u> a long time?
R: Yes, I (1) _____ (have) him (2) _____ ten years.
I: And how long (3) _____ (you live) in this apartment, Mr Bolton?
R: (4) _____ April 15th.
I: And your wife? How long (5) _____ (she be) in the USA?
R: (6) _____ last September.
I: And how long (7) _____ (you know) your wife?
R: (8) _____ six months.
I: And you (9) _____ (be) married (10) _____ February. Is that right?
R: Yes, we (11) _____ .
I: And your wife (12) _____ (not be) to the UK (13) _____ last September?
R: No, she (14) _____ .

8 📼 Listen and check. Then practise in pairs.

Get talking

9 In groups of 4, roleplay an immigration interview.

Students A and B: Turn to page 86.
Students C and D: Turn to page 89.

Language to go

A: How long have you lived here?
B: Oh, I've only been here for a few days.
A: Really? I've been here since 1880.

> GRAMMAR REFERENCE PAGE 117
> PRACTICE PAGE 108

Vocabulary   Nouns and verbs: word building
Function   Making and responding to suggestions
Language to go   Suggesting solutions to problems

Problem solving

Vocabulary

1 Complete the sentences with nouns made from the verbs in brackets. Use a dictionary to help you.

Example:
I had a <u>visit</u> from my boss when I was in hospital. (to visit)

1 Did you get an _____ to Mick's dinner party? (to invite)
2 I was so angry about the food that I made a _____ to the manager. (to complain)
3 We need a _____ to this problem. Any ideas? (to solve)
4 He says he's 40 but that's a _____ . He's 48. (to lie)
5 Adam had a good _____ . He said we should sell the company. (to suggest)

2 🔲 **Listen and repeat the nouns. Where is the stress on words that end in -tion?**

Listening

3 🔲 **Listen and match the pictures with the situations.**

4 **Listen again to Jack and Becky and answer the questions.**

1 When did Dan arrive?
2 How long did Jack invite Dan to stay for?
3 What do Jack and Becky want Dan to do?
4 What suggestions do Jack and Becky make?

Ⓐ

5 **Listen again to Tom and Jane and answer the questions.**

1 What's Tom and Jane's problem?
2 Did Tom talk to his neighbour about the problem?
3 What suggestions do Tom and Jane make?

Language focus

6 **Look at the examples below and match the two halves of these explanations.**

1 We use *Why don't we* / *Shall we* / *Let's* with
2 We use *What about* / *How about* with

a) the *-ing* form.
b) the infinitive (without *to*).

Making suggestions		Responding to suggestions
Why don't we *Shall we*	*tell* him the truth?	(+) *That's a good idea.* *That's not a bad idea.*
Let's sell the flat.		(−) *I don't think that's a very good idea.*
What about *How about*	*asking* him to dinner?	

39

Get talking and writing

9 In pairs, discuss problems and make suggestions.

1 Read and discuss the problem situations below. Write down the suggestion you both think is the best for each situation.

Why don't we ... ?
Shall we ... ?
How / What about ...ing?
Let's ...

2 Give your suggestions to another pair of students.

3 Read the suggestions you receive and write a response for each one. Then give them back to the original students.

Situation A You and your partner have decided to have a dinner party. Your friends, Richard and Judy, recently got divorced and they really don't like each other. By mistake, one of you has invited Richard and the other has invited Judy. You don't want to upset them, but it will be difficult if they both come to the party.

Situation B Your 50-year-old uncle and aunt are coming to visit you and your partner for the day. Think about the area where you live and plan what you are going to do with them.

Practice

7 Complete the suggestions on the left with *How about*, *What about*, *Let's*, *Why don't we* or *Shall we*. Then match them with the responses on the right.

1 <u>How about</u> buying a new computer?
2 _____ eat outside this evening?
3 _____ ask Dad for some money.
4 _____ paint this room yellow?
5 _____ asking Tim to help us?
6 _____ inviting the neighbours to the party?

a) No. He hasn't got any.
b) Good idea. I love that colour.
c) No, this one is fine.
d) That's a nice idea, but I think it's going to rain.
e) That's not a bad idea. Then we can make a lot of noise.
f) He can't. He's too busy.

8 In pairs, practise the dialogues.

Language to go

A: Shall we go out for a meal?
B: I haven't got any money.
A: How about asking your brother for some?

> GRAMMAR REFERENCE PAGE 117
> PRACTICE PAGE 109

Vocabulary Parties
Grammar Second conditional (*if* + past simple + *would* / *could*)
Language to go Talking about imaginary situations

Celebrate

Vocabulary

1 **Put the words in the box in the correct column.**

soft drink a live band fancy dress beach
alcohol-free beer rock dinner jazz salsa
wine champagne birthday lager

Drink	Party	Music
soft drink		

2 **Complete the sentences with words from Exercise 1.**

Example: I wore a policeman's uniform to the <u>fancy dress</u> party.

1 There's a _____ band playing at the pub tonight, but I prefer salsa or jazz.
2 Have you got any _____ for the children? A cola or something?
3 No, I can't have a normal beer. I'm driving. Have you got any _____ ?
4 I don't have _____ parties because I can't cook.
5 What _____ would you like to drink, red or white?
6 It's Jan's _____ party on Saturday. She's 21 years old.

Reading

3 **Read the advert and answer the questions.**

1 Why is the magazine having a competition?
2 What do you have to do?
3 What's the prize?
4 How old do you have to be to enter the competition?

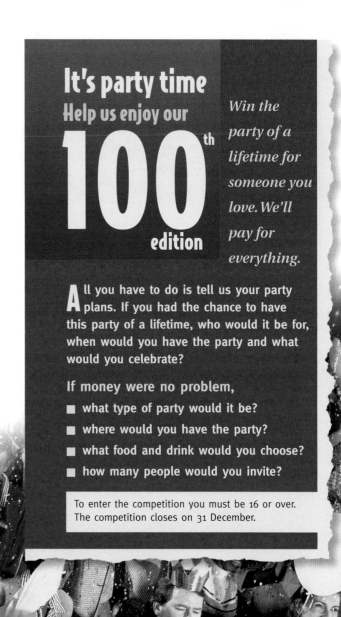

It's party time
Help us enjoy our
100th
edition

Win the party of a lifetime for someone you love. We'll pay for everything.

All you have to do is tell us your party plans. If you had the chance to have this party of a lifetime, who would it be for, when would you have the party and what would you celebrate?

If money were no problem,
■ what type of party would it be?
■ where would you have the party?
■ what food and drink would you choose?
■ how many people would you invite?

To enter the competition you must be 16 or over.
The competition closes on 31 December.

40

4 Match the sentences with A or B above.

Example: If we had a formal dinner party with the family, my parents would love it. *B*

1 I'd have a party on a yacht if money were no problem.
2 If it were possible, I'd have fireworks.
3 I'd take them to a special restaurant if I had the money.
4 They wouldn't like it if they had to sit down to eat.
5 If I had a live band, everyone would dance.
6 If the children didn't come, it wouldn't be such a family occasion.

Grammar focus

5 Look at the examples below and <u>underline</u> the correct word in the explanation.

We use the second conditional to talk about *real /
imaginary* situations.

Second conditional

(+) *If* I *had* a live band, everyone *would dance*.
I*'d have* a party on a yacht *if* money *were** no problem.

(−) *If* the children *didn't come*, it *wouldn't be* such a family occasion.
They *wouldn't like* it *if* they *had to sit down* to eat.

(?) *If* you *had* a party for your friends, where *would* it *be*?

* We can use *were* or *was*.

---

6 [cassette] Listen and practise the examples above, using contracted forms.

Practice

7 Use the prompts to make second conditional sentences.

Example: I haven't got enough money so I won't go on holiday.
If I had enough money, I'd go on holiday.

1 Lenny works in London so he lives there, but he wants to live in the country.
2 I have a sister so I have to share a bedroom.
3 She wants to give up work, but she can't because she needs the money.
4 Jacob has three children so he has a car, but he really wants a motorbike.
5 You don't use your computer very often so I don't send you e-mails.

Get talking

8 Enter the competition advertised and choose a winner.

1 In pairs, discuss what to write on the entry form.

2 Tell other students what you have decided.

3 Vote for the winning entry.

Language to go

A: What would you do if you won a million dollars?
B: If I won all that money, I'd go on holiday.

> GRAMMAR REFERENCE PAGE 117
> PRACTICE PAGE 109

Lesson 13, Exercise 9, Group A

1 **Use the prompts to make questions to ask Group B. Use the correct form of *have* or *have got* in your questions.**

  1 city / 56 museums and galleries?
    a) Amsterdam
    b) San Francisco
    c) Sydney

    Example: Which city has got 56 museums and galleries?

  2 restaurants / Hard Rock Café? (in the world)
    a) 112
    b) 438
    c) 209
  3 underground system / 4.3 million passengers a day?
    a) Moscow
    b) New York
    c) Lisbon
  4 restaurant chain / restaurants in 57 countries?
    a) Hard Rock Café
    b) Burger King
    c) McDonald's
  5 city / 274 underground stations?
    a) London
    b) Madrid
    c) Paris
  6 restaurant chain / 4,500,000 customers a day?
    a) Hard Rock Café
    b) Burger King
    c) McDonald's

2 **Check the answers:**

  1 b) 2 a) 3 b) 4 b) 5 a)
  6 c)

3 **Ask Group B your questions. Count the number of correct answers they get.**

Lesson 21, Exercise 7, Group A

1 **With another student from Group A, discuss and write down the part of the story where Grace killed Jim Stewart. Use the phrases marked * in your story.**

  1 Describe the hotel room Jim Stewart was in.
  2 What was he doing when Grace took him the whisky?
    * She didn't say anything to him but,
  3 What was Grace thinking about when she gave him the poisoned whisky?
    * Grace left the room immediately.
  4 What was Grace doing when Jim Stewart drank the whisky?
    * After ten minutes, Grace went back to his room.
  5 What did Grace say to Jim Stewart when he was dying?

2 **Work with a student from Group B. Put your parts of the story together. Then read them to another pair of students.**

Lesson 23, Exercise 7, Student A

Describe these objects for Student B to guess.

(I think) it's / they're made in / of ...
You wear them on your ... / You use them to ...

- Calvin Klein underwear
- BMW cars
- Coca-Cola bottles
- Benetton sweaters

Lesson 27, Exercise 9, Group A

You are a patient.

1 Think of a medical problem then visit three or four doctors (students from Group B). Tell them what the matter is and how you feel.

  Example: I've got a backache and it's very difficult to walk. I feel very depressed because I have to stay at home all the time.

2 Tell the class about your consultations. Who was the best doctor? Did you get any worrying or surprising information?

Lesson 28, Exercise 8, Student A

With Student B, take turns to describe things in your pictures. Find six more changes.

The picture opposite is of the room before the 'Changing Rooms' team has changed it.
Student B's picture is of the room after the changes.

Example:
A: The walls in my room are white.
B: In my room, they're green.
A/B: So they've painted the walls green.

Lesson 29, Exercise 9, Student A

1 **For each situation, imagine your partner is the person <u>underlined</u> and ask him / her for permission.**

   1 You missed your train and you need to phone for a taxi. <u>Your friend</u> has a mobile phone.

   2 You're in a café. There are four of you but there are only three chairs round the table. <u>The person at the next table</u> is alone and there are extra chairs round his / her table.

   3 Your friend is coming to visit you and he / she has a lot of luggage. <u>Your sister / brother</u> has a car. You want to borrow it so you can meet your friend at the airport.

   4 You're on a train. The window is open and you're cold. There's <u>a stranger</u> sitting opposite.

2 **Listen to your partner. Use these prompts to respond.**

   1 Give permission.
   2 Refuse permission because you're trying to study.
   3 Give permission.
   4 Refuse permission because you left it at home.

Lesson 30, Exercise 8, Pair A

1 **In pairs, think of three alternatives for each situation. Use vocabulary from Exercise 1 to help you.**

   Example: You met your boyfriend / girlfriend two months ago. You love him / her but he / she cannot stay in your country because of visa problems.

   Would you:
   a) *end the relationship?*
   b) *move to your boyfriend / girlfriend's country?*
   c) *marry him / her so he / she could stay in your country?*

   1 You are at a restaurant with three friends. You find $200 on the floor.
   Would you: a) ?   b) ?   c) ?

   2 Your sister says, 'My husband is going to phone you. Please tell him I was with you last night.' She wasn't with you.
   Would you: a) ?   b) ?   c) ?

2 **Ask and answer your questions with Pair B.**

Lesson 31, Exercise 9, Student A

1 **Read the text and write questions about the missing information.**

Example: *What was stolen from a train?*

In 1963 in the UK, (1) _____ was stolen from a train. The crime was known as the Great Train Robbery. The train was stopped near (2) _____ . The driver was attacked and the train was then driven (3) _____ along the line. 120 bags of banknotes were taken to a farm and (4) _____ was shared between the train robbers. But very soon, most of the criminals were arrested and they were sent (5) _____ .

2 **With Student B, ask and answer your questions.**

Lesson 38, Exercise 9, Students A and B

1 **You are a married couple.**

B is from another country. Immigration officers are going to interview you and you have five minutes to prepare for the interview. Work together to make sure you give the same information about:
- how long B has been in the country
- how long you've known each other
- where you met
- your wedding
- your jobs
- what you do in your free time

2 **Student A: Answer Student C's questions.**
Student B: Answer Student D's questions.

3 **Discuss your interviews. Do you think you gave the same answers?**

Lesson 32, Exercise 1

KEY
Mainly **a)** answers: You have very little willpower. Try harder!
Mainly **b)** answers: You have a lot of willpower. Well done!
Mainly **c)** answers: You have some willpower but not enough. Don't give up!

Lesson 13, Exercise 9, Group B

1 **Use the prompts to make questions to ask Group A. Use the correct form of *have* or *have got* in your questions.**

1 restaurants / Burger King? (in the world)
  a) 8,500
  b) 4,900
  c) 11,188
  Example: *How many restaurants has Burger King got in the world?*

2 city / 700 live music events every week?
  a) Lisbon
  b) Mexico City
  c) London

3 city / 5 airports?
  a) London
  b) New York
  c) Warsaw

4 city / 1000 mm of rain per year?
  a) St Petersburg
  b) Barcelona
  c) Mexico City

5 restaurant chain / 15,000,000 customers a day?
  a) McDonald's
  b) Hard Rock Café
  c) Burger King

6 stations / New York underground (subway)?
  a) 345
  b) 468
  c) 842

2 **Check the answers:**

1 c)   2 c)   3 a)   4 c)   5 c)
6 b)

3 **Ask Group A your questions. Count the number of correct answers they get.**

Lesson 21, Exercise 7, Group B

1 **With another student from Group B, discuss and write down the end of the story, where we learn what happened to Grace. Use the phrases marked * in your story.**

  1 What was the doctor doing when Roddy phoned him?
  The doctor went immediately to the police station and

  2 What did the doctor give Grace?
  Grace soon stopped crying and

  3 What was Grace doing when Roddy and the doctor went to the hotel?
  They climbed the stairs and

  4 Where was Jim Stewart lying when Roddy and the doctor went into his room?

  5 Did Roddy and the doctor tell anyone about the murder?

  6 What happened to Grace?

2 **Work with a student from Group A. Put your parts of the story together. Then read them to another pair of students.**

Lesson 23, Exercise 7, Student B

Describe these objects for Student A to guess.

(I think) they're made in / of ...
You wear them on your ... / You use them to ...

- Gucci bags
- Tag Heuer watches
- Levi jeans
- Nikon cameras

Lesson 24, Exercise 3, Student B

1 **Read about 'Phantom of the Opera' and complete your part of the table.**

	The Mousetrap	Phantom of the Opera
1 date of first performance	1952	1986
2 type of show		
3 how it ends		
4 reasons for popularity		

2 **Ask Student A about 'The Mousetrap' and complete the table.**

Phantom of the Opera

ANDREW LLOYD WEBBER is the most successful writer of musicals in the UK and 'Phantom' is his most successful musical. Since it opened in London in 1986, Her Majesty's Theatre has never had an empty seat.

The Phantom is a young composer with an ugly face. He hides his face behind a mask and lives in the Paris Opera House. He falls in love with a beautiful opera singer called Christine, but the opera singer loves Raoul. The Phantom makes her choose: 'Come with me and Raoul lives. Choose Raoul and he dies.' She goes with the Phantom, but in the end he helps Christine and Raoul to stay together.

Audiences love the costumes, the scenery, the story and the music. ▯

Lesson 27, Exercise 9, Group B

You are a doctor.

1 Three or four patients (students from Group A) will come and visit you. You have a maximum of two minutes per patient. Listen to their problems and give them advice.

You should ...

2 Tell the class about your patients. Which patient had the most worrying / interesting / surprising symptoms?

Lesson 28, Exercise 8, Student B

With Student A, take turns to describe things in your pictures. Find six more changes.

The picture above is of the room after the 'Changing Rooms' team has changed it.
Student A's picture is of the room before the changes.

Example:

B: *The walls in my room are green.*

A: *In my room, they're white.*

A/B: *So they've painted the walls green.*

Lesson 29, Exercise 9, Student B

1   **Listen to your partner. Use these prompts to respond.**

1   Give permission.
2   Refuse permission because you're waiting for some friends.
3   Refuse permission because you need it to get to work.
4   Give permission.

2   **For each situation, imagine your partner is the person underlined and ask him / her for permission.**

1   You are going to your friend's party and you would like to stay for the night because your last train home is at 11 p.m.

2   You want to watch television. Your flatmate is reading.

3   You need to leave the lesson early because you have a doctor's appointment. Your teacher is quite strict.

4   You are in an English lesson and you need a dictionary. You think your partner has one.

Lesson 30, Exercise 8, Pair B

1 **In pairs, think of three alternatives for each situation. Use vocabulary from Exercise 1 to help you.**

Example: You met your boyfriend / girlfriend two months ago. You love him / her but he / she cannot stay in your country because of visa problems.

Would you:
a) *end the relationship?*
b) *move to your boyfriend / girlfriend's country?*
c) *marry him / her so he / she could stay in your country?*

1 Your younger brother wants to take ten friends to your Mediterranean villa for a holiday. You know they will make a terrible mess. Would you: a) ?   b) ?   c) ?

2 Your uncle works for a computer company and says he can get you a well paid job there. You are no good with computers but you need to earn more money. You have a friend who is very good with computers. Would you: a) ?   b) ?   c) ?

2 **Ask and answer your questions with Pair A.**

Lesson 31, Exercise 9, Student B

1 **Read the text and write questions about the missing information.**

Example: *What was the crime known as?*

In 1963 in the UK, £2 million was stolen from a train. The crime was known as (1) _____ . The train was stopped near London. The (2) _____ was attacked and the train was then driven one kilometre along the line. (3) _____ bags of banknotes were taken to a farm and the money was shared between the train robbers. But very soon, (4) _____ were arrested and they were sent to prison.

2 **With Student A, ask and answer your questions.**

Lesson 38, Exercise 9, Students C and D

1 **You are immigration officers.**

A and B are married. B is from another country and you don't think it's a real marriage. You are going to interview the couple and you have five minutes to prepare for the interview. Work together to prepare questions to ask them. You will ask both A and B the same questions, about:
- how long B has been in the country
- how long they've known each other
- where they met
- their wedding
- their jobs
- what they do in their free time

2 **Student C: Ask Student A your questions.**
Student D: Ask Student B your questions.

3 **Compare A and B's answers. Are they telling the truth?**

89

Practice

1 A life of achievement

Vocabulary: regular and irregular verbs

1 Match a verb in A with two words / phrases in B.

Example: *can > swim / play football*

A	B
1 be	a) ten years old / single or married
2 have (got)	b) play the piano / dance
3 can	c) chocolate / my friend
4 like	d) three brothers / a car

2 Write questions. Use these prompts and the correct form of a verb above.

Example: What / your name?
What's your name?

1 / you swim?
2 / you married?
3 How many brothers and sisters / you / ?
4 / you / Madonna?
5 How old / you?
6 / you play the guitar?
7 / you / a flat or a house?

Grammar: past simple

3 Complete each gap with the correct past simple form of the verb in brackets.

The entrepreneur, Anita Roddick, <u>was</u> (be) born in Britain in 1942. She (1) _____ (start) the first 'Body Shop' in 1976 in Brighton.

She (2) _____ (not have) experience of running a cosmetic shop but she (3) _____ (have) lots of good ideas. She (4) _____ (want) to 'make profits with principles'; she (5) _____ (not want) to use cosmetics tested on animals. She (6) _____ (give) fair money to all her employees, including people from poor countries. By 1993, Anita Roddick (7) _____ (be) one of the five richest women in the world.

But her principles (8) _____ (be) still important to her. In November 1999, she (9) _____ (work) with other protesters in Seattle to fight the World Trade Organisation. In the year 2000 she (10)_____ (decide) to leave the world of business to be a full-time campaigner on social issues.

2 Billy Elliot

Vocabulary: free time activities

1 Find the activity which does not usually go with the word on the left.

Example: to – run, dance, <u>football</u>
(*play* <u>not</u> *to* football)

1 *play* – gymnastics, volleyball, golf
2 *do* – ballet, yoga, run
3 *to* – golf, run, box
4 *play* – football, golf, ballet
5 *do* – yoga, swim, gymnastics

Grammar: likes / dislikes + *-ing* form

2 Look at the grid. Then add the correct name and write a complete sentence from the prompts.

	boxing	football	gymnastics	ballet
Jo	– –	++	–	+
Pam	– –	+	++	–
Dave	++	+	–	
Ed	–	+	– –	++
Lou	–	++	+	– –

KEY ++ really love / enjoy / like   + quite enjoy / like
– not enjoy / like very much   – – really hate

Example: really like / play / football but he / not enjoy box / very much.
Lou really likes playing football but he doesn't enjoy boxing very much.

1 really hate / box / but he quite like / do / ballet.
2 quite like / play / football and he really enjoy / do / ballet.
3 really enjoy play / football and he quite enjoy / do / gymnastics.
4 quite enjoy play / football and she really hate / box.
5 really hate do / ballet but he really love / boxing.

3 Correct the five mistakes.

Example: Charlie and Mike both like (go) to   *going* the cinema and watch (1) good films. They enjoy going out with friends but Charlie prefers go (2) out on Saturday because he is tired in the week, after work. He is usually stay (3) in and watches TV. Mike go (4) out every night. He loves going to the gym but he doesn't like play (5) sports.

3 Hurricane

Vocabulary: weather, seasons and clothes

1a) Complete the puzzle.
b) What word is in the central column?

> *Clues*
>
> Example: You ski on this. *snow*
>
> 1 You wear this on your head when it's sunny.
> 2 We write –19°. We say _____ nineteen degrees.
> 3 When the temperature isn't cold but it isn't really hot.
> 4 We write 30°. We say thirty _____ .
> 5 The thing you wear round your neck.
>
> | | s | n | o | w | |
> 1 _ _ _ _ _ _
> 2 _ _ _ _ _
> 3 _ _ _ _ _ _
> 4 _ _ _ _ _ _ _
> 5 _ _ _ _ _

Grammar: present simple and present continuous

2 Underline the correct verb form.

Example: **Are you leaving?** / Do you leave now?

1 Today I *am wearing / wear* shorts but I usually *am wearing / wear* jeans.
2 *Are you usually having / Do you usually have* lunch at 1 p.m.?
3 Look. Pat *isn't wearing / doesn't wear* a sunhat and it's really hot.
4 John is *talking / talks* to someone over there.
5 Gill *isn't always walking / doesn't always walk* to work.
6 Paul *is never watching / never watches* TV.
7 *Are you knowing / Do you know* my wife?
8 He *isn't sleeping / doesn't sleep*. He's in the kitchen.

3 Change the sentences to questions and write short answers.

Example: I live in Seattle. (✔)
Do you live in Seattle? Yes, I do.

1 You work in a bank. (✔)
2 They're doing the shopping. (✔)
3 Carol usually gets home before 7 p.m. (✘)
4 It's snowing. (✘)
5 We're leaving now. (✔)
6 Susan and Francis often visit you on Sunday. (✘)
7 You know my address. (✘)
8 Michael's having a bath. (✔)

4 Possessions we hate

Vocabulary: possessions

1 Arrange the dominoes and find the names of six possessions.

Grammar: possessive's, adjectives and pronouns

2 Complete the chart.

subject pronoun	possessive adjective	possessive pronoun
I	my	mine
you	*your*	
	her	
he		
		ours
they		

3 Read about Paul and Jane. Then complete the sentences and say who things belong to.

Example: It's **Paul and Jane's** flat. It's **Paul's** camera.

1 It's _____ cat.
2 It's _____ car.
3 It's _____ mobile.
4 It's _____ hi-fi.
5 They're _____ magazines.
6 They're _____ glasses.
7 They're _____ CDs.

> Paul and Jane live in a small flat in London with their cat, Smokey. Paul is a photographer. He drives to work every day. Jane only drives their car at the weekend. She always takes her mobile with her. She usually goes to the tennis courts and plays tennis. Paul stays at home and reads photography magazines. He wears glasses but only for reading. When Jane comes home she usually listens to music. She's got a big collection of CDs, and she and Paul have got an excellent hi-fi.

4 Rephrase each sentence above twice. Use a possessive adjective and a possessive pronoun.

Example: It's Paul and Jane's flat.
It's their flat. It's theirs.

5 A Scottish wedding

Vocabulary: weddings

1 Look at the photo. Rearrange the letters and label the people.

oomrg

ebdir *bride*

egtsu

nmstbea

dsmrbdiaei

Grammar: *should / shouldn't* and imperatives

2 Correct the doctor's advice for a healthy life. Use imperatives or negative imperatives.

Example: You should smoke. *Don't smoke.*

1 You shouldn't drink lots of water.
2 You should stay up late at night.
3 You shouldn't eat lots of vegetables and fruit.
4 You should drink lots of coffee or tea.
5 You should sit in front of the computer all day.

3 Complete the sentences with *should* or *shouldn't* and one of these verbs.

wear go read buy wash be speak

Example: My hands are dirty. I **should wash** them.

1 He _____ without his glasses. He'll get a headache.
2 You are tired. You _____ to bed early tonight.
3 We _____ English in class.
4 It's cold. They _____ shorts.
5 That jacket is old. You _____ a new one.
6 She _____ unkind to her brother.

6 Travel with English

Vocabulary: countries and continents

1 Complete the crossword with names of countries.

Clues
1 Nelson Mandela was in prison in this country.
2 A Latin American country beginning with C.
3 The country where the composer Chopin was born.
4 Dublin is the capital of this country.
5 Go here to see the Taj Mahal.
6 This country has two official languages: French and English.
7 A country famous for pizza and pasta.
8 What's this word?

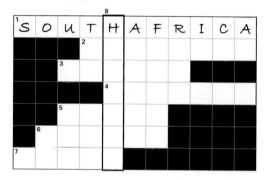

Grammar : the future with *going to*

2 Look at the pictures and complete sentences to say what people are going to do.

Example: She is / She's going to watch TV.

1 They
2 He
3 We
4 You

3 Match clauses from A and B to complete the sentences.

A
1 Kenny isn't going to buy a new car
2 Paula's going to leave her job
3 I'm not going to lend Jenny any money
4 We're going to have a dinner party on Saturday

B
a) and we'd like you to come.
b) because she never pays people back.
c) because she hates it.
d) because he hasn't got enough money.

7 Why women iron

Vocabulary: adjectives to describe character

1 Match the two halves to make words.

Example: hardw orking

1 talk | 2 aggres | 3 ti | 4 compe | 5 coope | 6 me

rative | dy | titive | sive | ssy | ative

2 Complete the sentence with a word from Exercise 1.

Example: Jim is so **hardworking** he doesn't have time to visit us.

1 Peter always wants to win. He's very _____ .
2 Ruth is a very _____ person. She always leaves her clothes on the floor.
3 Richard never speaks but his brother is the opposite. He's very _____ .
4 Stop fighting! I hate this _____ behaviour.
5 Lucy is a very _____ person. She never leaves her room in a mess.
6 Can't you be _____ just for once and help me?

Grammar: comparatives

3 Read the letter. Only one comparative form is correct. Correct the nine mistakes.

> Dear Brad,
> I'm in love. My new girlfriend is much
> nice than Carol. (nicer)
> I'm much (1) happy now. She isn't
> (2) as more talkative as Carol and she
> is (3) more good at listening. She's
> (4) as taller as Carol and she's
> (5) more beautiful than Carol. The only
> problem is she is (6) as worse as me
> at cooking so I'm a lot (7) thin now
> than I was before.
> You must meet her soon.
> Well the other news is that yesterday
> I bought a new car. It's (8) more fast
> than the old one and is (9) more easy
> to drive. Of course it wasn't as
> (10) cheaper as the last car but I
> love it... nearly as much as Carol!

8 Take a risk

Vocabulary: adventure sports

1 Write the name of the sport in each picture.

Example: snowboarding

Grammar: present perfect and past simple

2 Use the prompts to write the questions for the answers.

Example: / you ever do / any rock climbing?
Have you ever done any rock climbing?

1 / Jack ever visit / Scotland? Yes, he has.
2 When / Susan first do scuba diving?
  In the year 2001.
3 / you study / in London before?
  No, I haven't. This is my first time.
4 / Ken ever live / in Africa?
  No. I don't think he has.
5 / we send a card to Dad last week? Yes, we did.
6 / Penny get that bag for her birthday?
  No. I don't think so.
7 / Helen and Lorrie buy their house last year?
  No, they didn't.
8 / you see / this video before? Yes, I have.

3 Complete the conversation with the words from the box.

> snowboarding have never diving
> haven't was ever did good went

TOM: Quick, Sam, look at these people
    snowboarding.
SAM: Fantastic. Have you (1) _____ done that?
TOM: No, I (2) _____ . Have you?
SAM: Yes, I (3) _____ .
TOM: Really? When (4) _____ you do that?
SAM: Oh, about four years ago. When I (5) _____
    to Sweden.
TOM: Was it (6) _____ ?
SAM: Yes. It (7) _____ great.
TOM: The most frightening thing I've done is scuba
    (8) _____ .
SAM: I've (9) _____ done that.

> For more exercises, go to www.language-to-go.com **93**

9 Job share

Vocabulary: at the office

1 Underline the noun in each group which does not usually go with the verb.

arrange – <u>an e-mail</u>, a meeting, an appointment

1 send   – a phone, a fax, a report
2 get   – a letter, an e-mail, a meeting
3 write   – a report, the photocopying, a letter
4 do   – the photocopying, a meeting, the report
5 answer – a letter, a phone, a report
6 have   – a meeting, the photocopying, an
            appointment

2 Complete the memo with the correct form of the verbs from Exercise 1. You may use these verbs more than once.

Dear Kenny,
   I <u>got</u> an e-mail this morning from Mr Bens. He asked me to photocopy the report and tell everyone they are
(1) _____ a meeting this week.
I've (2) _____ the photocopying and I've (3) _____ all the e-mails, but I didn't have time to
(4) _____ a meeting with Mr Sykes for Thursday at 10 a.m.
   I'll (5) _____ a fax to the managers and invite them to the New Year party but could you (6) _____ Penny an e-mail? She never
(7) _____ her phone and she says she never (8)_____ my letters.
Thanks. Hope you have a good day.
Cheers, Linda

Language focus: offers and requests

3 Correct the mistake in each sentence.

Example: Can you send this e-mail Jim, please?
Can you send this e-mail **to** Jim, please?

1 I meet you at the station tonight.
2 Can you send the information me, please?
3 Can you pass to me the milk, please?
4 Shall you carry this for me, please?
5 I help you.
6 Can you answer me the phone, please?
7 Shall I to get you a newspaper?
8 You can open the memo for me, please?

10 Behave yourself

Vocabulary: verbs and their opposites

1 Write five more pairs of verbs under the pictures.

| give borrow send lend get forget |
| push remember take come pull go |

Example:

a come   b go   1 a _____ b _____
2 a _____ b _____   3 a _____ b _____
4 a _____ b _____   5 a _____ b _____

Thanks– I'll return it later.

Grammar: zero conditional

2 Write complete sentences. Use the zero conditional and the person in brackets.

Example: If / get / headache / go / bed early. (I)
If I get a headache, I go to bed early.

1 If / come / London / usually stay / with me. (Jo)
2 If / smile at people they often smile back. (you)
3 She get / angry if / forget / birthday. (we)
4 If / get / letter every week / be / happy. (they)
5 / go / cinema if / have / time at / weekend. (she)

3 Match two clauses to make complete zero conditional sentences.

Example: If Jack gets angry *everybody leaves.*

1 If you ask a question
2 She takes the train
3 They don't always dance
4 If he wants a cigarette
5 If we need a drink
6 You feel terrible

a) if you stay up late every night.
b) do we ask the waiter?
c) if they go to a club.
d) if she misses the bus.
e) they always answer.
f) can he smoke outside?

11 Customs change

Vocabulary: customs

1 Complete the sentences with the correct form of the verb.

wear (x 2)   stay   play   take   open   have

Example: He usually <u>takes</u> his jacket off in the house.

1 I _____ a dress to the party last night.
2 My hands are full. Can you _____ the door for me, please?
3 I _____ breakfast in bed yesterday.
4 I never _____ jeans to work.
5 Let's _____ at home tonight.
6 We _____ a game of cards yesterday evening.

Grammar: *used to / didn't use to*

2 Look at the pictures and write sentences with *used to*.

Example: I *used to eat meat but now I only eat vegetables.*

12 Win some, lose some

Vocabulary: shops and purchases

1 Reorder the letters. What did Daniel buy?

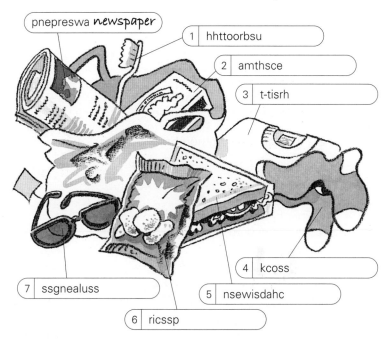

pnepreswa *newspaper*

1 hhttoorbsu
2 amthsce
3 t-tisrh
4 kcoss
5 nsewisdahc
6 ricssp
7 ssgnealuss

2 Daniel bought two things from each place. Match the things above to the places below.

Example: a café – *crisps and sandwiches*

a) a clothes shop
b) a newsagent's
c) a chemist's

Grammar: *because / for /* infinitive of purpose

3 Write the best ending for each sentence.

Example: I'm going to the garage <u>b</u>.

a) to catch a train   d) to open the door
b) to get some petrol   e) to invite him out
c) to wash   f) to watch the football

1 They phoned Tom _____ .
2 Do you need a key _____ ?
3 We went to the station _____ .
4 He got up late so he didn't have time _____ .
5 They turned on the TV _____ .

4 Complete each gap with *to*, *for* or *because*.

Example: She went to the restaurant <u>to</u> have a meal.

1 He visited his grandmother _____ it was her birthday.
2 We are going to the park _____ a walk.
3 I want to see you _____ we need to talk about the meeting.
4 Shall we go to France _____ a holiday?
5 Do you need some money _____ buy food?

13 The Ritz

Vocabulary: large numbers

1 Write the following as numbers.

Example: Two thousand and fifteen = *2015*

1 four hundred and ninety-eight
2 sixty-five thousand four hundred and ten
3 six thousand and thirty-seven
4 a hundred and fifty-two
5 five million four hundred thousand
6 nine thousand and forty-one

2 Find the missing number.

Example: twenty-nine + *50* = *79*

1 a hundred and fifteen + ? = 480
2 a hundred x ? = 2,600
3 Four hundred and sixty-seven – ? = 439
4 Three hundred and sixty ÷ ? = 60

Glossary			
+	plus	–	minus
x	times / multiplied by	÷	divided by

Grammar: *have* and *have got*

3 Complete the dialogues with *have / has / haven't / hasn't*, *do / does* and *don't / doesn't*. Use contractions where possible.

Example:
A: **Have** you got an alarm clock I can borrow, please?
B: Yes, I **have**. I'll get it for you now.

1 A: _____ John and Jane have lunch here?
   B: No, they usually _____ it at the pub.
2 A: I _____ got any money. Will you lend me some, please?
   B: I'm sorry. I _____ only got £1 and I need it.
3 A: _____ Peter have the address of the hotel?
   B: Yes, he _____ , but I don't know what it is.
4 A: _____ Paula got my CD?
   B: No, she _____ . I think Dan _____ got it.

4 Use the prompts to make questions. Write questions with both *have* and *have got* where possible.

Examples: / you / a swimming pool?
Do you have a swimming pool?
Have you got a swimming pool?

1 / you / a car?
2 / they always / coffee after a meal?
3 / that hotel / many visitors each month?
4 / you / a headache?
5 / you / any money?
6 / Tom sometimes / milk in his tea?

14 Food for thought

Vocabulary: food and drink

1 Put the letters in the correct order to make names of food and drink.

Example: tsla > *salt*

3 eeelvtgasb
6 rteaw
4 cuetlet
8 ksecoio
5 iuecj
1 rrrsseewtabi
2 nsoino
7 rgouyt

Grammar: *some, any, much, many, a lot of*

2 Play a memory game.

a) Look at the picture for two minutes then cover it. Use the words in the box and write questions about the tray. Use *was / were* like this:

Was there any orange juice on the tray?

| 1 coffee? 2 biscuits? 3 sugar? 4 fruit? |
| 5 sandwiches? 6 cakes? 7 milk? 8 tea? |

b) Answer your questions in complete sentences. Then look at the picture again and check.

Example: *There wasn't any orange juice on the tray.*

3 Write a question beginning *How much?* or *How many?* for each sentence.

Example: I read a lot of books last week.
How many books did you read?

1 I bought some t-shirts yesterday.
2 I took a lot of photos on holiday.
3 I drank a lot of wine last night.
4 I wrote some postcards in Spain.
5 I watched a lot of videos at the weekend.
6 I listened to some CDs on my walkman.
7 I put a lot of sugar in your tea.
8 I ate a lot of fruit yesterday.

15 A nice place to work

Vocabulary: clothes

1 Write both the American and British English words for each picture.

American English   British English
sweater   jumper

Grammar: *have to*

2 Complete the dialogues with the correct form of *have to* and *do*.

Example:
A: you (get up) early this morning?
  Did you have to get up early this morning?
B: Yes, I *did*.

1 A: _____ you (work) this evening?
  B: Yes, unfortunately I _____ .
2 A: _____ Thomas (wear) a uniform at his last school?
  B: No, he _____ .
3 A: _____ Sara (wear) a suit at the office?
  B: No, but I _____ .
4 A: _____ Tim (drive) to work?
  B: No, he _____ but he prefers driving to walking.
5 A: _____ I (finish) this report now? I'm not well.
  B: Well you _____ (finish) it before Friday.
6 A: Peter _____ (leave) now.
  B: No, he _____ (not leave) until 9.30 a.m.

3 Rewrite the sentences so they have the same meaning.

Example: It's necessary for Sam to go to hospital.
Sam has to go to hospital.

1 It's necessary for him to work at the weekend.
2 It isn't necessary for us to call him now.
3 It wasn't necessary for us to wear a uniform at school.
4 Was it necessary for you to work last Saturday?
5 It's necessary for Jason to phone his parents when he gets here.
6 Is it necessary for me to have a visa?

16 Mumbai soap

Vocabulary: topics for TV soaps

1 Put two of the words below under each topic.

cricket husband marriage football
theft prison passion parents

love	crime	sport	family
marriage			

Grammar: future predictions with *will / won't*

2 Use *will / won't* + one of these verbs to complete each gap in the horoscope.

wake up be make worry move
speak fall feel love have

You **will be** very lucky next month. Your stars (1) _____ into the best position possible and you (2) _____ any problems. You (3) _____ in love with a tall dark stranger and this person (4) _____ you in return. You (5) _____ lots of money and you (6) _____ about anything. You (7) _____ more and more confident. You (8) _____ one morning and you (9) _____ fluent English.

3 Look at the underlined words. Choose the correct question word and write the question for each prediction.

Example: You will work for three years *in a bank*.
Where will I work?

1 You will start work *in January*.
2 You will meet *interesting new people*.
3 You will fall in love with *a tall dark stranger*.
4 You will get married *in Paris*.
5 You will have *three* children.
6 You will live *in a big house*.
7 You will earn *a lot of money*.
8 You will *travel* around the world.

17 Camden Market

Vocabulary: adjectives describing places/objects

1 Match each definition with the correct adjective in the box.

second-hand   busy   attractive
popular   trendy   unknown

Example: A place (or person) full of activity. **busy**

1 This place or person is good to look at.
2 People like this thing or person very much.
3 Someone bought these clothes, books or furniture before you.
4 Nobody has heard of this person or thing.
5 This describes fashionable clothes, things or people.

Grammar: superlatives

2 Complete the gaps in the chart.

adjective	comparative	superlative
quiet	quieter	the quietest
new		
big		the biggest
busy	busier	
popular		the most popular
	better	the best
bad		the worst

3 Write sentences with comparatives and superlatives.

Example: Carina is <u>smaller</u> than Amanda. Belinda is <u>the tallest</u>. Carina is <u>the smallest</u>. (tall /small)

I'm Belinda. I'm 30. Some people like me.

I'm Amanda. I'm 25. Everybody likes me.

I'm Carina. I'm 20. Nobody likes me.

1 Amanda is _____ Carina. Belinda is _____ . Carina is _____ . (old / young)

2 Belinda is _____ Amanda. Carina is _____ . Amanda is _____ . (happy / sad)

3 Belinda is _____ Carina. Amanda is _____ . Carina is _____ . (popular / unpopular)

18 On the move

Vocabulary: travel

1 Match each verb in A with two nouns it can go with in B. Use each verb and pair of nouns once only.

Example: **get + a visa / a certificate**

A	B
1 renew	a) a suitcase / a bag
2 rent	b) a passport / a visa
3 pack	c) money / a bank account
4 book	d) a car / a flat
5 transfer	e) a hotel room / a ticket

2 Complete notices with the correct verb above.

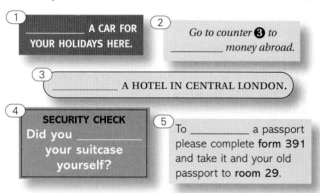

① _____ A CAR FOR YOUR HOLIDAYS HERE.

② Go to counter ❸ to _____ money abroad.

③ _____ A HOTEL IN CENTRAL LONDON.

④ SECURITY CHECK Did you _____ your suitcase yourself?

⑤ To _____ a passport please complete **form 391** and take it and your old passport to **room 29**.

Grammar: present perfect with *yet* and *already*

3 Look at the list of holiday preparations. Write your mother's questions to find out what you and your flatmate Sarah have done so far.

Example: rent flat (me ✔)
Have you rented the flat yet?
Has Sarah booked ...?

TO DO BEFORE WE GO FOR A WEEK IN THE COUNTRY
1 rent car (me ✔)
2 book hotel (Sarah ✗)
3 cancel newspapers (me ✗)
4 ask neighbour to feed cat (me ✗)
5 buy new bag (Sarah ✔)
6 pack case (me ✗)
7 clean house (Sarah ✗)
8 do food shopping (me ✔)
9 pay telephone bill (Sarah ✔)
10 phone for taxi to airport (me ✗)

4 Write a response for each sentence. Use present perfect + *already* or *yet*.

Example: I've already rented the flat.

19 Real fighters

Vocabulary: sports

1 Find each instructor's sport / activity, hidden in their name.

Example: H. I. Dringrose = *horseriding*

SPORTS CENTRE

Room number	instructor's name
1	N.U. Grinn
2	K.I. Sing
3	C.C. Nigly
4	Nic Gand
5	X. Bingo
6	Ian Tring
7	Ms. Win Gim
8	Thin Figg

2 Complete each gap in these definitions with the name of the person or verb in the same word family.

Example: A *horserider* rides a horse.

1 A _____ skis.
2 A runner _____ .
3 A boxer _____ .
4 A _____ trains other sports people.
5 A _____ dances.
6 A swimmer _____ .
7 A cyclist _____ .
8 A _____ fights.

Grammar: past abilities and adverbs of degree

3 Put these words in the correct order. Make sentences about people's past abilities.

Example: play the well guitar couldn't very I
I couldn't play the guitar very well.

1 very artist well draw could This
2 boxing at good The young were men quite
3 sing very well couldn't I
4 you Were at French speaking good?
5 We were could ski when we young well
6 wasn't dancing very good She at
7 swim He well couldn't very
8 were playing good really They musical instruments at

20 The message behind the ad

Vocabulary: adjectives in advertised products

1 Underline the adjective which does not usually go with the noun.

Example: teeth – reliable clean white

1 orange juice – fresh healthy soft
2 hair – shiny delicious soft
3 clothes – soft clean healthy
4 coffee – delicious fresh reliable
5 car – reliable fresh fast

Grammar: first conditional

2 Use the prompts to make first conditional sentences.

Example: You should take the medicine. (If not)
_____ / your cold / get worse
If you don't take the medicine, your cold will get worse.

1 You should use this shampoo. If _____ / your hair / be soft and shiny.
2 You shouldn't drink a lot of coffee. If _____ / you / not sleep.
3 You should try this coffee. If _____ / you / love it.
4 You should go to bed now. If / not _____ / you / feel tired tomorrow.
5 You should eat more fruit. If _____ / you / not get ill.
6 You should stop smoking. If _____ / you / feel better.
7 You should study more. If not _____ / you / not pass your exam.
8 You shouldn't buy that coat. If _____ / you / not have any money to buy the jeans.

3 Put the verbs in the correct form to complete the dialogues.

Example:
A: What she (do) if she (get) ill?
  What **will she do** if she **gets** ill?
B: If she (get) ill, she (find) a doctor.
  If she **gets** ill, **she'll find** a doctor.

1 A: But what (happen) if she (lose) her passport?
  B: Well, if she (do), she (go) to the Embassy.
2 A: If Jack (be) late, you (get) angry?
  B: No, but if he (be) late, I (not wait) for him.
3 A: If Nancy (lose) her money, what she (do)?
  B: She (call) us if that (happen).
4 A: If Pat (ask) you to her party, you (go)?
  B: Yes. And if I (go), you (come) with me?

21 The story of Grace

Grammar: past simple and past continuous

1 Look at the pictures and word prompts and write sentences using the past simple and past continuous.

Example: **It was raining when he left the house.**

| rain | leave / the house | Peter / talk / Tim | see / an accident |
| I / have / bath | I / you phone / me | We / watch / video | everything / suddenly / go / black |

2 Choose the best verb form.

Example: Last Saturday was a beautiful day. It was warm and the sun *shone* / *was shining* so Helen went for a walk.

Helen (1) *walked* / *was walking* in the park when she (2) *saw* / *was seeing* something which (3) *made* / *was making* her very angry. In the street just outside the park a man (4) *shouted* / *was shouting* at a woman. The woman (5) *cried* / *was crying* but the man (6) *didn't stop* / *wasn't stopping*. Helen immediately (7) *ran* / *was running* to help the woman. When she got to the woman Helen (8) *started* / *was starting* to laugh because she (9) *heard* / *was hearing* another man say, 'OK stop. Let's do that again.' Helen (10) *realised* / *was realising* that the people (11) *acted* / *were acting*. They (12) *made* / *were making* a film.

3 Use the prompts to make questions for each answer.

Example: What / Helen see when she / walk / in the park?
What did Helen see when she was walking in the park?
She saw something which made her very angry.

1 What / the man do / when Helen see / him?
He was shouting at a woman.
2 What / the woman do / ? She was crying but the man didn't stop.
3 Why / Helen laugh? She realised the people were acting.
4 What / the people do / ? They were making a film.

22 Just the job for you

Vocabulary: jobs

1 Which description do you not usually associate with each job?

Example: chef is creative / works with people / ~~travels a lot~~.

1 farmer	works outside / is creative / works with animals
2 barman	works alone / doesn't earn a very good salary / works inside
3 mechanic	works with machines / works with animals / has dirt on his work clothes
4 pilot	doesn't travel very often / earns a good salary / has a lot of responsibility
5 market researcher	works with people / has a lot of responsibility / works with animals

Grammar: *would like to* + infinitive / *like* + *-ing*

2 Complete the dialogues with *would / wouldn't / do / does / don't / doesn't*.

Example: Do you like taking photographs?
Yes I **do**. I **would** like to be photographer.

1 A: (1) _____ Jane like swimming?
B: Yes, she (2) _____ .
A: (3) _____ she like to come with us on Friday?
B: I'm sure she (4) _____ .
2 A: (1) _____ you like to be a politician when you're older?
B: No. I (2) _____ like talking to big groups of people.
3 A: (1) _____ you like to live in England?
B: No, I (2) _____ . I hate cold, wet weather.
A: (3) _____ you like going to very hot countries?
B: Yes, I (4) _____ . I (5) _____ like to live in Australia or Indonesia.
4 A: (1) _____ Nick and Jeremy like playing football?
B: Nick (2) _____ but Jeremy (3) _____ .
A: Do you think Nick (4) _____ like to play on Sunday?
B: I don't know. Ask him.

3 Use the prompts to make full sentences.

1 Would Tom like / be a pilot?
2 Does Helen like work / with children?
3 Do Sam and Fran like act / ?
4 Would you like / do a more creative job?
5 Do you like work / with Harry?

23 Made in the USA

Vocabulary: materials and possessions

1 Find a word in each column to describe each picture.

Example: 2 – *wooden box*

number	material	object
2	wooden	ashtray
	metal	socks
	leather	box
	cotton	jacket
	glass	fork
	gold	tray
	silver	pen

Grammar: present simple passive

2 Change active sentences into passive sentences.

Example: They make Scotch whisky in Scotland.
Scotch whisky is made in Scotland.

1 They make Nissan cars in Japan.
2 They sell stamps in a post office.
3 Where do they sell this Scandinavian furniture?
4 Do they sell Spanish oranges in British supermarkets?
5 They don't make these earrings out of gold.
6 They sell Brazilian coffee all over the world.
7 They make leather jackets in Turkey.
8 Do they buy a lot of chocolate in Belgium?

3 Choose the correct form, active or passive, in these sentences.

Example: Beautiful silver jewellery *is made* / makes in Chile.

1 They *are sold* / sell perfume at the chemist's.
2 A lot of tea *is bought* / buys in China.
3 Glass *is made* / makes from sand.
4 They *are bought* / buy all their clothes in France.
5 They *aren't sold* / don't sell cigarettes in this shop.
6 Milk *is bought* / buys directly from the farm.
7 They *are made* / make delicious food in that restaurant.
8 Money *is bought and sold* / buys and sells every day on the stock market.

24 A long run

Vocabulary: the theatre

1 Look at the picture and label with words from the box.

> stage   actors   singer   game
> chairs   audience   musical   seats

Grammar: *a / an* and *the*

2 Describe the picture above. Complete each gap with *a*, *an*, *the* or one of the words in the box in Exercise 1.

Last night we went to see **a musical** at the Queen's Theatre in town. We had (1) _____ most expensive (2) _____ in the theatre. We were really near (3) _____ (4) _____ and we could see all (5) _____ (6) _____ really well. One group sat on (7) _____ and played (8) _____ (9) _____ of cards. (10) _____ best moment was when (11) _____ (12) _____ sang the final song. (13) _____ (14) _____ clapped and clapped.

3 Choose *a / an* or *the*.

Example: There was _a_ / the cat and _a_ / the dog in the room. A / _The_ dog's name was Fido.

1 This morning I bought *an* / the apple and *a* / the banana for lunch. I ate *an* / the apple but I didn't eat *a* / the banana.
2 A: Have you got *a* / the car?
   B: No, I haven't got *a* / the car but I've got *a* / the bicycle.
3 We went out for *a* / the meal on Saturday. A / The restaurant was really good and *a* / the food was excellent. I had *a* / the best fish I've ever eaten.
4 They live in *a* / the house in *a* / the country. There is *a* / the beautiful garden behind *a* / the house and *a* / the big veranda at *a* / the front.

> For more exercises, go to www.language-to-go.com   **101**

25 Smart agreements

Vocabulary: verb and noun combinations

1 Choose the correct verb.

Example: Did you *do* / *make* the housework before you went to work?

1 He was sorry to *lose* / *forget* your birthday. He won't do it again.
2 If we *make* / *do* an agreement not to talk about it, I promise I won't.
3 I often *forget* / *lose* my temper when I'm tired.
4 You shouldn't *do* / *make* a fuss every time you visit them.

Grammar: *have to, don't have to, mustn't*

2 Complete the questions with the correct form of *have to*.

1 When / we / leave the party?
2 How much / you / pay for a taxi?
3 What do you / do at work tomorrow?
4 Why / Pat / visit his grandparents?
5 How long / you / wait for the bus?
6 What time / I / phone you this evening?

3 Rephrase these notices using *mustn't*.

Example: You mustn't smoke.

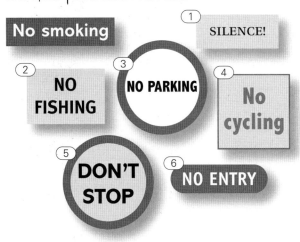

4 Complete with *mustn't* or *don't have to / doesn't have to*.

Example: Now I work from home I *don't have to* get up early.

1 You _____ feed bread to the goats. They get ill if you give them bread.
2 You _____ forget to phone her. It's important.
3 We _____ leave yet. We have lots of time.
4 He's got a beard so he _____ shave.
5 She's very rich so she _____ work.
6 I _____ wear a jacket to work but I usually do.
7 You _____ tell anyone. It's a secret.

26 Australian barbecue

Vocabulary: food

1 Put the torn-up shopping list back together again.

Example: straw berries

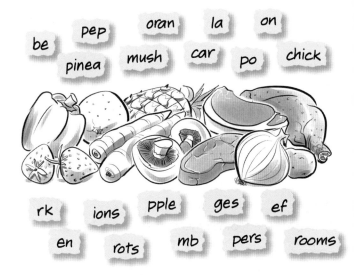

Grammar: *going to* and *will*

2 Complete these dialogues with the correct form of *be going to* or *will*. Use contracted forms if possible.

Example:
A: *Are you going to* (you) visit Mary this evening?
B: Yes. *I'm going to* drive there at about six o'clock.
A: Good. *I'll* come too. I haven't seen her this week.

1 A: What _____ (you) buy Vanessa for her birthday?
  B: I'm not sure. I think I _____ get her some flowers.
  A: That's a good idea. I _____ choose a pretty vase to go with them.

2 A: Jane and I _____ watch TV this evening.
  B: Oh, I think I _____ join you.
  A: Ok, but come early. We _____ (not) stay up late. We _____ have an early night.

3 A: How _____ (you) travel to the airport on Sunday?
  B: Pete _____ take me by car.
  A: Lucky you. Do you think I can come with you?
  B: I _____ ask him.

27 Irritating illnesses

Vocabulary: medical symptoms; the body

1 Find ten parts of the body in the word snake. They are all interconnected.

Example: (b a c(k)n e(e)l b o w) = back + knee + elbow

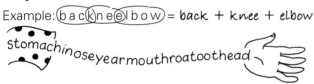
stomachinoseyearmouthroatoothead

2 Put letters in order to make names of illnesses.

Example: ahtotceoh = toothache

1 hbcaceak   4 ldco   6 haracee
2 asrh   5 hsocmacahet 7 rose trhota
3 hhedacea

Grammar: adjectives ending in *-ed* and *-ing*

3 Underline the correct adjective.

Example: The football match was very excited / exciting.

1 The film was really *bored / boring*.
2 I used to be *frightened / frightening* of the dark.
3 These symptoms are very *worried / worrying*.
4 She was *surprised / surprising* to see her father.
5 You should read that book. It's very *interested / interesting*.
6 She was very *depressed / depressing* after she had the baby.
7 I was *shocked / shocking* to hear he was so ill.
8 The silence was *embarrassed / embarrassing* but things soon went back to normal.

4 Form the correct adjective from the noun in brackets.

Example: He was very **depressed** when he lost his job. (depression)

1 (boredom)   **The film was so _____ I nearly went to sleep.**

2 (shock)   The violence in this film is quite _____ .

3 (surprise)   *You will be _____ by the ending of this film. It's quite extraordinary.*

4 (fright)   **Horrific! Very _____ . You won't sleep at night.**

5 (depression)   Everyone in the film seemed sad and _____ .

6 (interest)   The idea was _____ but it didn't really work.

28 Changing rooms

Vocabulary: furniture and fittings

1 Do the puzzle. What word does 10 down make?

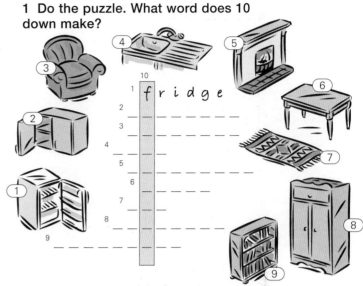

Grammar: present perfect for present result

2 Use the prompts under each picture to complete each sentence. What has happened in each one?

Example: **The young woman has bought a dress.**

buy / dress   win / race   have / accident

not / go / out   see / film   break / plate

paint / room   go / sleep   not / finish / food

1 The runner _____ .   5 The child _____ .
2 Charlie _____ .   6 The couple _____ .
3 The woman _____ .   7 Grandpa _____ .
4 They _____ .   8 The cat _____ .

29 How rude!

Vocabulary: table manners

1 Look at the pictures. Describe what the person is doing in each picture.

Example: He's got his feet on the seat.

Language focus: permission

2 Match a question to a response.

Example: 1 – f)

A
1 Is it OK if Kim stays here tonight?
2 Can I borrow your umbrella, Jane?
3 Is it OK if I stay out late tonight?
4 Is it OK if I leave my car here?
5 May I close the window? I'm a bit cold.
6 Is it OK if Simon borrows your car?

B
a) Please do. I'm cold too.
b) Yes, sure. Park it behind mine.
c) I'm sorry, I need it. I'm going out now, myself.
d) OK, but no later than midnight.
e) No, it isn't. Why can't he get the bus?
f) Yes, of course. She can sleep in your room.

3 Find the mistake in each dialogue and correct it.

A: Is OK if I use your mobile phone?
   Is it OK if I use your mobile phone?
B: Yes, of course. Here it is. (*This is correct.*)

1 A: Can I to leave early?
   B: I'm sorry but I need you here until 8 p.m.

2 A: Could I keep these books for three weeks?
   B: Certainly. I'm afraid, you can only have them for two.

3 A: Is it OK I close the curtains?
   B: Yes, certainly. The sun is in my eyes, too.

4 A: May I use your phone?
   B: No, of course. I'm waiting for a call.

30 What would you do for love?

Vocabulary: verbs and their opposites

1 Choose the correct opposites for the verbs below from the box.

> lend   tell the truth   agree   find
> get married   stay   sell   go

Example: borrow – lend

1 come   5 lie
2 move (to)   6 buy
3 lose   7 get divorced
4 refuse (to do something)

2 Use some of the verbs from Exercise 1 to complete the sentences. Use the correct form of the verb.

Example: I left my dictionary at home.
Can you **lend** me yours, please?

1 I haven't got a pen. Can I _____ yours, please?
2 I'm going to _____ my CD player. I want $150 for it.
3 I'm so happy that she _____ to see the doctor. I was worried.
4 _____ me the truth. Did you really miss the train?
5 I asked John to help me, but he _____ .
6 That's their old address. They've _____ to Ireland.
7 Oliver always _____ about his age. He isn't 25. He's 30.
8 I can't leave the country. I _____ my passport.

Grammar: *would* + infinitive (without *to*)

3 Put the words in italics in the correct order.

Example:
A: you / that / hat / would / wear?   B: Yes. It's great.
Would you wear that hat?

1 *buy / 'd / I / jacket / that*. It's a beautiful colour.
   _____

2 A: *lend / a / you / stranger / would / money / some*?
   B: No, I wouldn't.
   _____

3 *n't / to / lie / my / would / I / friends*. Would you?
   _____

4 *would / move to / Prague / n't / they*.
   They couldn't leave their family.
   _____

5 *you / that / much / spend / money / would / a car / on*? I wouldn't.
   _____

6 *would / Janet / me / the truth / tell*. She's my friend.
   _____

31 The art of crime

Vocabulary: Crime

1 Complete the TV crime report with a noun or the correct form of the verb in brackets.

Example: (shoplift) _Shoplifting_ is now a big problem in London. Every day more and more _shoplifters_ are caught.

1 (rob) There was another bank _____ last night. Can you help us to find two bank _____ who _____ Bingley's Bank in Market Street?
2 (burgle) Thank you for your phone calls about the _____ last week. Because of the information you gave us the police caught the _____ .
3 (murder) There was a _____ last night. Can you help the police to find the person who _____ these two men outside a restaurant in Kings Road? The police think the _____ is someone who was at the restaurant that evening.

Grammar: past simple passive

2 Choose the correct form of the verb.

When I was young my sisters and I usually saw / were seen my grandparents every weekend. We really (1) enjoyed / were enjoyed our visits. When the weather was fine our grandparents (2) took / were taken us to the beach near their house. One Saturday we went for a swim and we (3) left / were left all our things on the beach and everything (4) stole / was stolen. We were very upset, but the next morning we (5) woke / were woken up very early by our grandparents and we (6) took / were taken to the shops. Our grandparents (7) bought / were bought us new CD players, new cameras and new watches – everything that (8) take / was taken by the thieves.

3 Complete the sentences with the past simple active or past simple passive form of the verb.

Example: Jack **bought** (buy) some shirts with the money he **was given** (give) for his birthday.

1 We (give) _____ the wrong address so we never (find) _____ the restaurant.
2 Mr and Mrs Smith (told) _____ the party (start) _____ at 8 p.m.
3 The teenagers (make) _____ so much noise they (ask) _____ to leave the cinema.
4 I (ask) _____ to give you a letter but I (lose) _____ it. Sorry.
5 The plane (cancel) _____ so we (give) _____ a free lunch.
6 Peter (give) _____ a new office but he (not like) _____ it.

32 Willpower

Vocabulary: phrasal verbs

1 Complete each thing on the list with the best verb from the box.

carry   give   cut   take   throw

NEW YEAR RESOLUTIONS

Give up chocolate.

1 _____ down on sugar.

2 _____ away old clothes.

3 _____ up Tai Chi classes.

4 _____ on doing exercises every morning.

Grammar: verbs and infinitive or -ing form

2 Make complete sentences from these word prompts.

Example: I / go / take up swim / next year.
I'm going to take up swimming next year.

1 Mary and John give up / smoke / three years ago.
2 I want / cut down / number of calories I eat.
3 / you go / carry on learn / Spanish after / holiday?
4 Lucy want / give up eat / chocolate but she can't.
5 We should carry on phone / her even if / not answer.

3 Choose the correct form of the verb.

Example: Do you enjoy to eat /(eating) in restaurants?

1 Do you want to see / seeing my brother?
2 He needs to visit / visiting a doctor urgently.
3 They gave up to wait / waiting for her.
4 They decided to phone / phoning home immediately.
5 Will you give up to smoke / smoking?
6 He didn't take up to dance / dancing until the year 2000.

> For more exercises, go to www.language-to-go.com   **105**

33 A typical day

Vocabulary: regular activities

1 Complete the sentences with the correct form of a verb from the box.

| spend   pay   make   empty   employ   do |

Example: Maria <u>spends</u> a lot of time with her children.

1 How many people do you _____ in your company?
2 Robin _____ the electricity bill at the end of last month.
3 Can I _____ a phone call, please?
4 Let's _____ the shopping now.
5 I _____ the rubbish every day.

Grammar: subject and non-subject questions

2a) Read the story. Who is late – Jack or Jane?

> ### Jack and Jane
>
> My sister Jane and I have an argument about the bathroom every morning. I like to sleep until about 8 a.m. and I get up at 8.15 a.m. This means I only have fifteen minutes to get ready before I leave the house to catch the 8.40 a.m bus to college.
>
> Jane always gets up about 6 a.m. and then she spends hours in the bathroom. I get really angry. Her classes don't start until 10 and she never leaves the house before 9.30 a.m., but she's always in the bathroom when I need it. Jane's never late for class. I'm late every day!
>
> Jane always tells me to get up earlier. I tell her to get her own bathroom. Then Mum tells us both to be quiet. Not a good way to start the day.

b) Use a verb from the box and the prompts below to form questions about the story.

| tell   get up (x2)   leave   get   catch   be   spend |

Example: Who / Jack and Jane to be quiet?
Their Mum.
Who tells Jack and Jane to be quiet?

1 When / Jack / ? 8.15 a.m.
2 Who / never late for class? Jane.
3 Who / the 8.40 a.m. bus? Jack.
4 Who / at 6 a.m.? Jane.
5 Why / Jack / angry? Because he can't get in the bathroom in the morning.
6 Who / hours in the bathroom? Jane.
7 When / Jane / the house? At 9.30 a.m.

34 How things work

Vocabulary: technical equipment

1 Name the pieces of equipment.

2 Match the definition to the equipment.

Example: A <u>laptop computer</u> has a screen and a keyboard and it's easy to carry around.

1 A _____ is a machine you use to talk to people and you can carry it with you anywhere.
2 A _____ copies texts and pictures into your computer.
3 A _____ copies texts and pictures from one piece of paper to another.
4 A _____ takes pictures but doesn't use a film.
5 A _____ prints things from your computer.
6 A _____ has a screen and a remote control.

Grammar: relative clauses

3 Complete each sentence with *who*, *that*, *which* or *where* and a word from the box.

| scarf   dictionary   photographer   dentist
airport   cooker   chef   digital camera   digital TV |

Example: A person <u>who</u> helps people with dental problems is called a <u>dentist</u> .

1 A system _____ lets you watch programmes when you want to is called a _____ .
2 A person _____ takes photographs is called a _____ .
3 A place _____ people catch planes is called an _____ .
4 A machine in your kitchen _____ cooks food is called a _____ .
5 A person _____ cooks food in a restaurant is called a _____ .
6 A book _____ has definitions of words is called a _____ .
7 A thing _____ you wear round your neck is called a _____ .
8 A machine _____ takes pictures without using a film is called a _____ .

35 What's that noise?

Vocabulary: sounds people make

1 Choose the best verb for each sentence.

Example: It was a very good show so we _clapped / yawned._

1 When her team won the football match Susie _yawned / cheered._
2 Louise _screamed / whistled_ when her brother hit her.
3 I was so tired that I _yawned / clapped_ all through the lesson.
4 I _cried / shouted_ because the film was very sad.

Grammar: present deductions with _must, might, can't_ + infinitive

2 Rewrite the first sentence with _must be_, _might be_ or _can't be_.

Example: I'm sure she isn't over 60 years old.
She goes running every day.
She can't be over 60 years old.

1 I'm sure she's Australian. Listen to her talking.
She _____ .
2 It's possible that he's asleep. I haven't heard any noise from his room.
He _____ .
3 I'm sure he isn't American. He's got an English accent.
He _____ .
4 I'm sure Jack is rich. Look at his new car.
Jack _____ .
5 It's possible that Ben is ill. He didn't go to work today.
Ben _____ .

3 Match the pairs of sentences.

Example: 1 – b)   2 – a)

1 They must be married.
2 They can't be married.

  a) He calls her his sister.
  b) They're called Mr and Mrs Smith.

3 Sam must be tired.
4 Sam can't be tired.

  a) He's yawning.
  b) He only got up ten minutes ago.

5 This must be Jill's coat.
6 This might be Jill's coat.

  a) But it looks too small for Jill.
  b) It's the only coat here.

7 It might be our bus stop.
8 This is our bus stop.

  a) Quick! Let's get off.
  b) Ask that man.

36 A football fan's website

Vocabulary: prepositions and times of the day

1 Complete the sentence with a preposition where necessary. X = no preposition.

Example: a) I went to the cinema **X** last night.
b) I went to the cinema **at** 8 p.m.

1 a) Did you buy any cheese _____ yesterday?
  b) Did you buy any cheese _____ Saturday?
2 a) Can you phone me _____ the evening?
  b) Can you phone me _____ this evening?
3 a) I have to go to the doctor's _____ next week.
  b) I have to go to the doctor's _____ 6 p.m.
4 a) Let's go out for coffee _____ the afternoon.
  b) Let's go out for coffee _____ tomorrow morning.
5 a) Henry came to see us _____ 1990.
  b) Henry came to see us _____ last month.

2 Correct the preposition mistakes in this e-mail.

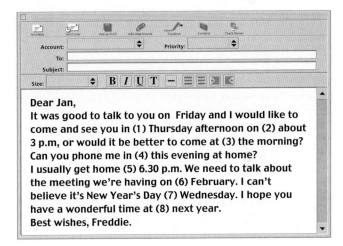

Dear Jan,
It was good to talk to you on Friday and I would like to come and see you in (1) Thursday afternoon on (2) about 3 p.m, or would it be better to come at (3) the morning? Can you phone me in (4) this evening at home? I usually get home (5) 6.30 p.m. We need to talk about the meeting we're having on (6) February. I can't believe it's New Year's Day (7) Wednesday. I hope you have a wonderful time at (8) next year.
Best wishes, Freddie.

Grammar: present continuous for future time

3 Use the prompts to make sentences and add a preposition if necessary.

Example: / you go / the football match / Saturday?
Are you going to the football match on Saturday?

1 / Ken come / to the party next Friday evening?
2 I / not go / to my Japanese lesson tonight.
3 / we have / spaghetti for supper this evening?
4 What / you do / Thursday evening?
5 Sue and Dan / not go / skiing January.
6 / Betty have / her driving test / Tuesday morning?
7 Ken and Mary / have lunch / at 1 p.m.
8 I / meet /Jo and Fred / Saturday evening.

37 It was so funny!

Vocabulary: adjectives and their opposites

1 Find opposites for these words below.

funny horrible mean full special ugly

I like it. It's great.

I don't like it. It's terrible.

great
generous
_____
attractive
_____
delicious
_____

terrible
_____
ordinary
_____
serious
_____
hungry

Grammar: *so / such* + adjectives / nouns

2 Underline *great* or *terrible*. Then choose the best word above to replace *great / terrible*.

Example: My uncle is really *great / terrible*. He always buys me expensive presents. *generous*

1 The food in that restaurant is *great / terrible*. I'm not eating there again!
2 Those clothes make you look really *great / terrible*. The blue matches your eyes.
3 I feel *great / terrible*. I haven't eaten since yesterday.

3 Complete each gap with *so* or *such*.

Example: The weather was *so* cold I needed a coat.

1 Everything is _____ expensive these days.
2 We had _____ a nice evening. Thank you very much.
3 They go straight home after work because they are usually _____ tired.
4 I've never heard _____ a stupid question.
5 Don't walk _____ slowly. We'll be late.
6 I couldn't finish it because it was _____ a boring book.

4 Rephrase these sentences. Change *so* to *such*, *such* to *so* and include the words in brackets.

Example: She is so nice. (person)
She is such a nice person.

1 The cake was so good. (It was …)
2 He was so tall. (man)
3 I was so surprised. (It was …)
4 It was such a strong wind. (The wind …)
5 The story was so long. (It was …)
6 You have such a lovely house. (Your house …)

38 Green card

Vocabulary: immigration

1 Rearrange the letters to make words.

Example: oimaigtinrm *immigration*

1 tmiepr   3 drca
2 svai   4 ceclein

2 Choose the correct word.

Example: I have to get a passport *photo* / *picture* for my new passport.

1 To get a job in America you need a green *permit* / *card*.
2 To drive a car you need a driving *permit* / *licence*.
3 In some countries you must have an identification *card* / *visa* with you all the time.
4 You often need a tourist *visa* / *permit* to travel to another country.
5 When you enter another country you have to go through *residence* / *immigration* where you show your passport.
6 When you work in another country you usually need a work *permit* / *licence*.

Grammar: present perfect with *for* and *since*

3 Use the prompts to make sentences with the present perfect. Add *for* or *since* where necessary.

Example: / you speak / to Joanna / last week?
Have you spoken to Joanna since last week?

1 I / know / Matt / 1980.
2 I / not have / this job / long.
3 Sally / not be / to London / 1999.
4 / you see / John / his birthday?
5 How long / you / have your driving licence?
6 We / not eat / any chocolate / ages.
7 They / not visit / Frank / June.

4 Write sentences which mean the same as these sentences. Use the verb in brackets with *for* or *since*.

Example: Pete moved to New York in 1998 and he still lives there. (live)
Pete's lived in New York since 1998.

1 Julian works at Ford. He started there two months ago. (work)
2 Susan's got a nice leather jacket. She bought it four years ago. (have)
3 We moved to this house in July. (live)
4 Peggy met David in 2000. (know)
5 Lucy got a new car. She got it on her birthday. (have)
6 I'm a teacher. I became a teacher in 1995. (be)
7 Lorna divorced Ian a few months ago. (be)

39 Problem solving

Vocabulary: word building

1 Complete the column with a verb or a noun.

noun	verb
solution	solve
	invite
visit	
	suggest
lie	
	complain

2 Complete the sentences with a word from Exercise 1 above.

Example: We must find a <u>solution</u> to this problem.

1 This food is terrible. I'm going to _____ to the manager.
2 Jack told me to change my job and I think that's a good _____ .
3 Did you get an _____ to Judy's party?
4 I know that's not true so don't _____ to me.
5 I'm going to _____ Mike in hospital.
6 We've had a lot of _____ about the receptionist. People say she is rude.
7 We have _____ two hundred people to our wedding.

Language focus: suggestions

3 Use the prompts to make suggestions.
1 What _____ (come) to visit me tonight?
2 Shall we _____ (send) your sister some flowers?
3 Why _____ you (buy) some new clothes?
4 It's late. How _____ (phone) for a taxi?
5 Let's _____ (invite) Kelly to dinner.
6 Why _____ we (complain) and get our money back?

4 Correct the mistakes in the sentences.

Example: Let not go out tonight.
<u>Let's</u> not go out tonight.

1 What about watch a video tonight?
2 Let's to stay at home this evening.
3 Is a nice idea.
4 Why we don't ask Lucy to help us?
5 How about to sell our old computer?
6 Shall we buying Sam a bike for his birthday?
7 I can't I too busy.
8 Why don't we going to bed early?

40 Celebrate

Vocabulary: parties

1 Look at the clues and complete the crossword.

Clues
1 It's a [bee] party.
2 [champagne bottle]
3 It's my _____ . I'm 27 years old today.
4 [drink being poured]
5 I listen to [musical notes] .
6 I'll have a glass of red [glass] .
7 I don't drink alcohol. Have you got a _____ ?
8 I like jazz but I don't like _____ music.
9 The name of a kind of music and a dance.

Grammar: second conditional

2 Use a second conditional to rewrite the first sentence. The meaning should be the same in both sentences.

Example: I don't know his phone number so I can't call him.
<u>If I knew his phone number, I'd call him.</u>

1 I don't know her e-mail address so I can't tell you.
2 She doesn't have enough money so she can't eat out tonight.
3 Kim doesn't study very hard so she won't pass her exam.
4 I don't do any sport so I'm not fit.
5 I feel tired so I can't play football today.
6 I haven't got my credit card with me so I can't buy that jacket.
7 I haven't got time so I can't help you.
8 I don't know his address so I can't invite him to the party.

> For more exercises, go to www.language-to-go.com

Grammar reference

Lesson 1

Past simple

- Use the **past simple** to talk about completed actions in the past, often with a time reference (**in 1990**, **yesterday, last year**, etc.):
  *She **started** her career as a TV newsreader in 2002.*
  *He **didn't see** her on Sunday.*
  *How **did** they **become** famous?*

  See the list of irregular verbs in the Phrasebook.

Lesson 2

Likes / dislikes + -*ing* form + qualifying adverbs

- Use a noun or the -*ing* form after these verbs: **like, don't like, love, enjoy, hate**:
  *I like **running**.*
  *He doesn't like **swimming**.*
  *Do you enjoy **dancing**?*
  *My children **love milkshakes**.*
  *We **don't like spiders**.*

- You can use **qualifying adverbs** (really, quite, very much, etc.) to express yourself more strongly:
  *I **really** love cooking!*
  *He **quite** likes spaghetti.*
  *She **really** enjoys playing tennis.*
  *We don't like running **very much**.*

> Note: These adverbs come before the main verb in the sentence, except for ***very much*** which comes at the end:
> *I don't like cooking **very much**.* NOT ~~I don't like **very much** cooking.~~

Lesson 3

Present simple and present continuous

- Use the **present simple** to talk about things that happen regularly …
  *It often **rains** in England.*
  *Tony **doesn't eat** chocolate.*
  ***Do** your friends often **go** to concerts?*

  … and to talk about things that are always true:
  *The moon **goes** round the sun.*

- Use the **present continuous** to describe things at this moment and around now:
  *Look! The sun's **shining**.*
  *He **isn't doing** his homework.*
  *What **are** you **doing**?*

- Use the **present simple** with these **verbs**: know, think, understand.
  *I **know** hurricanes **are** dangerous.*
  NOT ~~I am knowing hurricanes are dangerous.~~

Lesson 4

Possessive 's

- Use possessive **'s** after people's names and singular nouns:
  *They're the dog**'s** toys.*
  *It's not Paul**'s** guitar.*
  *Is that James**'s** car?*

- Use **'** after regular plural nouns:
  *That's her parents**'** house.*
  *These are the boys**'** mini-disks.*

- Use **'s** after irregular plural nouns:
  *The children**'s** toys.*
  *The men**'s** cars.*
  *The women**'s** books.*
  *People**'s** problems.*

Possessive adjectives

- Use possessive **adjectives** (my, your, his, her, its, our, their) to replace the noun in a sentence:
  This is Paul's guitar.   *It's **his** guitar.*
  That is the dog's bed.   *That is **its** bed.*

> Note: it's = it is (short form)   Its = possessive adjective

Possessive pronouns

- Use possessive **pronouns** (mine, yours, his, hers, ours, theirs) to replace possessive adjectives and nouns:
  They're my books.   *They're **mine**.*
  It's our house.   *It's **ours**.*

belong to

- Use the verb ***belong to*** to describe your possessions:
  The book belongs to me.
  NOT ~~I belong to the book.~~

  Belong to cannot be used in the continuous form:
  *The guitar **belongs** to Paul.*
  NOT ~~The guitar is belonging to Paul.~~

Lesson 5

should / shouldn't and imperatives

- Use **should** and **shouldn't** (without *to*) to ask for and give advice. Use **should** to say something is a good idea, and **shouldn't** to say it's a bad idea:
  *Should he wear jeans?   No, he **shouldn't**.*
  ***Shouldn't** we take a present?*
  *You **shouldn't** give them money.*
  *You **should** buy her some flowers.*

  You can use **imperatives** to give advice too:
  ***Don't arrive** late!*
  ***Be** polite to the groom's parents.*
  ***Sit** down.*

Lesson 6

The future with *going to*

- Use *be* + *going to* + infinitive to talk about future plans:

  Positive
  *I'm **going to** go to the Rockies in November.*
  *She's **going to** spend two months in South Africa.*
  *We're **going to** learn to water-ski.*

  Negative
  *I'm **not going to** go to the play tonight.*
  *He **isn't going to** spend the money he won last week.*
  *They **aren't going to** get married this year.*

  Question
  *Are you **going to** write a letter to him?*
  *Is he **going to** play tennis tonight?*
  *Are they **going to** get a dog?*

Lesson 7

Comparatives

- Use the **comparative form** of adjectives with **than** to compare two things:
  *It's **bigger than** my town.*
  *The climate is **drier than** in England.*

  Add **r** to one syllable adjectives ending in a vowel:
  large, larger

  Add **er** to one syllable adjectives ending in a consonant:
  cheap, cheaper

  Double the consonant and add **er** to one syllable adjectives ending in consonant + vowel + consonant:
  fat, fatter

  Change **y** to **i** + **er** to two syllable adjectives ending in **y**:
  heavy, heavier

  Add **more** to two or more syllable adjectives:
  beautiful, more beautiful

Irregular
bad, worse
good, better

- Use **not as** + adjective + **as** to say that there is a difference between two people or things:
  *John **isn't as** hard-working **as** you are.*
  (You work harder than John.)
  *Girls **aren't as** messy **as** boys.*
  (Boys are messier than girls.)

- Use **as** + adjective + **as** to say that there is no difference between two people or things:
  *I'm **as** tall **as** you are.*
  (We are the same height.)

Lesson 8

Present perfect and past simple

- Use the **present perfect** (**have** + past participle) to talk about experiences up to now. It isn't important when the experiences happened:
  *I've **acted** on television.*
  (At some time in my life. It doesn't matter when.)
  *Have you ever **been** to Switzerland?*
  (At any time in your life?)
  *Sophie **has** never **eaten** chocolate.*
  (Never in her life.)

- Use the **past simple** to talk about completed actions in the past, often with a time reference (**yesterday, last year**, etc.):
  *I **went** rock climbing a lot **when I was young**.*
  (A past action. I don't go now.)
  ***Did** you **finish** reading it?*
  (Action finished in past?)

Lesson 9

Offers and requests

- Use **will** in positive statements and **shall** in questions to offer to do things for people:
  I'll send the faxes for you.
  ***Shall** I book a restaurant?*

- Use **shall** in questions only with **I** and **we**:
  Shall I make some coffee?
  Shall we help you with that?
  NOT Shall he photocopy that?

- Use **can** and **could** (*which is slightly more formal than can*) to ask people to do things for you:
  ***Can** you photocopy this, please?*
  ***Could** you answer the phone?*

- Use **can I?** to offer to help someone:
  Can I carry your bags for you?

Lesson 10

Zero conditional (*if* + present form + present form)

- Use the **zero conditional** to talk about things that are usually true:
  If I forget a friend's birthday, I say sorry.
  If you go out in the rain, you get wet.
  If you don't charge the battery, it runs out.
  Does the car run better if you put in unleaded fuel?

> Note: The *if* clause often comes first but it can come second:
> *If I need money, I borrow it.   I borrow money if I need it.*
> See Lesson 20.

When the **if** clause comes first, put a comma after it. You don't need a comma when it comes second.

Lesson 11

Used to / didn't use to

- Use *used to* + infinitive to talk about things that happened a number of times in the past but don't happen now:
  I used to drink a lot of coffee.
  (But now I don't.)
  Women didn't use to smoke in public.
  (But now they do.)
  Peter didn't use to play football but he plays it now.
  Not didn't used to …
  Did you use to read a lot when you were a child?
  Not Did you used to …?

- Use the past simple for a completed action in the past:
  I drank a lot of coffee yesterday.
  Amanda smoked all my cigarettes last night!

Lesson 12

Because, for and infinitive of purpose (with *to*)

- Use **because**, **for** or an infinitive of purpose to answer the question **why** or **what for**:

  because + clause
  I went to the bank because I needed some money.

  for + noun
  I went to the bank for a new cheque book.

  infinitive with **to** + verb or noun
  I went to the bank to collect my credit card.
  NOT I went to the bank for to collect my credit card.

Lesson 13

Have and *have got*

- Use *have* or *have got* to talk about possessions:
  I have a dog and a cat.
  I've got a dog and a cat.
  We don't have many CDs.
  We haven't got many CDs.
  Do they have any brothers or sisters?
  Have they got any brothers or sisters?

- Use *have* to talk about routines or regular activities:
  I often have fruit for breakfast.
  NOT I often have got fruit for breakfast.
  She doesn't have milk in her coffee.
  Do they usually have toast?
  Yes, they do. / No, they don't.

> Note: In American English *Do you have …?* is more common than *Have you got …?*

Lesson 14

Some, any, much, many, a lot of

Have some bread or some biscuits.
I don't eat much chocolate or many cookies.
Do you have any milk?
We eat a lot of fruit and vegetables.

Countable and uncountable nouns

- Use *some* in positive statements when you don't know the exact quantity or it isn't important:
  I've got some bread.
  We bought some apples.

- Use *any* in negative statements and questions:
  He didn't get any cheese.
  Did we buy any oranges?

- Use *a lot of* to talk about a large quantity:
  We eat a lot of fresh fruit.
  I put a lot of vegetables in this dish.
  Do you drink a lot of water?
  I don't eat a lot of sweet things.

Countable nouns

- Use **many** in negative statements and questions:
  I don't eat many vegetables.
  How many tomatoes are there?
  Are there many apples?

Uncountable nouns

- Use **much** in negative statements and questions:
  *I don't spend **much** money.*
  *How **much** milk is there?*
  *Is there **much** yoghurt?*

Lesson 15

Past and present obligation with *have / had to*

Present

- Use *have / has to* to say that something is necessary:
  *I **have to** go to work today.*
  (I haven't got a choice.)

- Use *don't / doesn't have to* to say that it isn't necessary:
  *I **don't have to** work today – it's Sunday.*
  (My office is closed on Sunday.)

Past

- Use *had to* to say that something was necessary in the past:
  *I **had to** go to the supermarket yesterday.*
  (I didn't have any food.)

- Use *didn't have to* to say that it wasn't necessary in the past:
  *I **didn't have to** go to work last week.*
  (It was a holiday.)

Lesson 16

Future predictions with *will / won't*

- Use *will* and *won't* to predict the future:
  *(I think) Sanjay **will** be the hero of the match.*
  (This is my opinion about a future event.)
  *He **won't** fight.*
  (This is what I know, based on fact.)

Note: Use *I don't think I'll* . . . NOT *I think I won't* . . .

Lesson 17

Superlatives

- Use the **superlative form** of adjectives to compare three or more things:
  *Camden has **the biggest** craft market.*
  *It's not **the best** place to visit.*
  *Is it **the easiest** place to get to?*

Add **st** to one syllable adjectives ending in a vowel:
large, the largest

Add **est** to one syllable adjectives ending in a consonant:
cheap, the cheapest

Double the consonant and add **est** to one syllable adjectives ending in consonant + vowel + consonant:
fat, the fattest

Change **y** to **i** and add **est** to two syllable adjectives ending in **y**:
heavy, the heaviest

Add **most** to two or more syllable adjectives:
beautiful, the most beautiful

Irregular
bad, the worst
good, the best

Lesson 18

Present perfect with *yet* and *already*

- Use the **present perfect** to talk about actions that begin in the past and have an effect on the present:
  *I've already **bought** a guide book.*
  (Here is the guide book.)
  *We **haven't rented** a car yet.*
  (We haven't got a car, but we will get one.)

- Use *already* when the action is completed:
  *I've **already** got the visas.*
  (Here are the visas.)

- Use *not yet* when the action is not completed but you think it will happen:
  *I **haven't** found my passport **yet**.*
  (But I will.)

- Use *yet* to ask whether an action is completed:
  *Is the insurance organised **yet**?*
  (Have we got insurance?)

Lesson 19

Past ability with *could* and *be good at*

- Use *could / couldn't* to talk about abilities in the past:
  *I **could** read when I was four.*
  *I **couldn't** speak Italian when I got my first job.*
  ***Could** you drive when you were eighteen?*

You can also use *was / were good at* and *wasn't / weren't good at* to talk about abilities in the past:
*Ali **was** really **good at** boxing.*
*James **wasn't good at** Maths.*
***Were** you **good at** sports?*

- Use **adverbs of degree** (quite, very, really) in positive statements to emphasise what you are saying:
  *I was **really** good at playing the piano.*
  *Paul was **quite** good at swimming but his brother was **very** good.*
  *James could swim **really** well when he was **very** young*
  *Were you **very** good at French?*

- Use **adverbs of degree** (very) in negative statements to emphasise what you are saying:
  *I wasn't **very** good at basketball.*
  NOT ~~I wasn't **really** good . . .~~ OR ~~I wasn't **quite** good . . .~~

Lesson 20

First conditional (*if* + present simple + *will*)

- Use the **first conditional** to talk about things that may or may not happen in the future:
  *If you **buy** this car, you**'ll meet** a beautiful woman.*
  (You may or may not buy this car.)
  *If you **don't hurry**, we**'ll be** late.*
  (You may or may not hurry.)
  *We**'ll repair** the machine if it **goes** wrong.*
  (The machine may or may not go wrong.)
  *If we **ring** you tonight, **will** you **be** in?*
  (We may or may not ring you.)

  *If + present, **will** / **won't** + infinitive.*

> Note: The *if* clause often comes first but it can come second:
> *If I lose weight, I'll be happy. I'll be happy if I lose weight.*
> When the *if* clause comes first, put a comma after it. You don't need a comma when it comes second.

Lesson 21

Past simple and past continuous

- Use the **past simple** and **past continuous** together in one sentence if the first action is still going on when the second action happens:
  *Sam **was climbing** the tree when Jim **came** out of the house.*
  (First Sam started climbing the tree; then Jim came out of the house.)
  *I **was talking** to Fiona when we **heard** the shot.*
  (First I started talking to Fiona; then we heard the shot.)
  *Tom **wasn't doing** his homework when his teacher **arrived**.*
  ***Were** the children **walking** the dog when it **disappeared**?*

Lesson 22

Like + *-ing* and *would like* + infinitive with *to*

- Use *like* + *-ing* form to talk about your present likes and dislikes:
  *I **like learning** new skills.*
  *I **don't like working** outside.*
  ***Do** you **like** that new boy band?*

- Use *would like* + *to* + infinitive to imagine future possibilities:
  *I**'d like to be** a teacher.*
  ***Would** you **like to write** books?*
  *I **wouldn't like to be** a farmer.*

Lesson 23

Present simple passive

- Use the **passive** when you are not interested in who does the action, or it isn't important who does it, or you don't know who does it:
  *The boxes **are made** in Hungary.*
  (It isn't important who makes them.)
  *Where **are** the boxes **made**?*
  *They **are sold** for $75 dollars.*
  (It isn't important who sells them.)
  *What **are** the boxes **made** of?*

  The **object** of an active sentence becomes the **subject** of the passive sentence:
  *People make **the boxes**.* (Active)
  ***The boxes** are made.* (Passive)

  To form the **present simple passive** use the present form of the verb **to be** + past participle:
  *The silver **is bought** in Mexico.*
  *The boxes **are made** in Hungary.*

Lesson 24

A / *an* and *the*

- Use *a* / *an* the first time you talk about something:
  ***A** young couple have **an** old house.*

- Use *the* when you talk about the same thing again:
  ***The** couple turn **the** house into a hotel.*

- Use *the* when there is only one example of something:
  ***The** moon goes around **the Earth**.*

- Use *the* with superlative adjectives:
  *'The Mousetrap' is **the longest-running** play in the world.*

- Don't use *the* when you are talking about things in general:
  I like ice cream.
  NOT I like the ice cream.
  Shirley loves music.
  NOT Shirley loves the music.

  But use *the* when you are talking about something specific:
  I don't like the ice cream they make at our local restaurant.
  Did you enjoy the music he was playing yesterday?

Lesson 25

Have to, don't have to, mustn't

- Use *have / has to* to say that something is necessary:
  John has to be home by ten.
  (That's what his father says.)
  Do I have to wait for you?
  (Is it necessary to wait?)

- Use *don't / doesn't have to* to say that it isn't necessary:
  You don't have to do the washing up.
  (We've got a dish-washing machine.)

- Use *mustn't* to say 'don't do it':
  You mustn't park here.
  (That's what the law says.)
  You mustn't eat those sweets.
  (That's what my mother says.)

Lesson 26

The future with *going to* and *will*

- Use *going to* + infinitive to talk about decisions you have made for the future:
  I'm going to buy some new books.
  I'm not going to see my grandmother tonight.
  Are we going to ring Peter?

- Use *will* + infinitive to make a decision at the time of speaking:
  What shall we have to eat?
  I haven't decided yet, er... OK, I'll make an omelette.
  What are we going to take?
  I don't know ... I've got an idea! We'll take sausages!

Lesson 27

Adjectives ending in *-ed* and *-ing*

- Use **adjectives ending in *-ed*** to describe the way you feel:
  Marisa is annoyed.
  Luke is shocked.
  They're frightened.
  Are you bored?

- Use **adjectives ending in *-ing*** to explain what or who makes you feel this way:
  Marisa is annoyed because she's just received an annoying email.
  Is Luke shocked because he's just read a shocking newspaper article?
  The film was frightening – the children were both frightened.
  I'm bored because this work is boring.

Lesson 28

Present perfect to describe present result

- Use the **present perfect** to talk about actions that happen in the past and have a result in the present:
  We've polished the floorboards.
  (The floorboards are shiny now.)
  He hasn't removed the fireplace.
  (It's still there.)
  Have they changed the sofa covers?
  (I think they were blue. They're red now.)

Lesson 29

Permission

- Use **can**, **could** and **may** to ask for permission to do something:
  Can I borrow your car?
  No, I'm sorry, you can't.
  Could I use your mobile, please?
  Yes, here you are.
  May I use your telephone?
  Of course you can.

  Note: *could* is more formal than *can*; *may* is more formal than *could*.

- Use **is it OK if** . . . in informal situations:
  Is it OK if I smoke? Yes, of course.

Lesson 30

Would + infinitive (without *to*)

- Use *would* + infinitive for imaginary situations:
  I would buy a large house in the country.
  She wouldn't tell anybody about it.
  Would you tell a lie? No, I wouldn't. / Yes, I would.

Lesson 31

Past simple passive

- Use the **passive** when you are more interested in the action than in the person or thing that did the action:
  Every day cars were stolen.
  (I don't know who stole the cars.)
  A window was broken.
  (I don't know who broke it.)
  When were the cars stolen?
  Which bank was burgled?

  If you want to say who did the action, use **by** + the person / thing:
  The manager was murdered by the robber.
  The building wasn't hit by lightning.
  What was the car hit by?

  The **object** of an active sentence becomes the **subject** of the passive sentence:
  Someone found my wallet. (Active)
  My wallet was found. (Passive)

  To form the past simple passive use the past form of the verb **to be** + the past participle:
  A copy of the painting was made.
  Several banks were burgled.
  The woman wasn't murdered.
  Were the videos found?

Lesson 32

Verbs with *-ing* form / infinitive (with *to*)

- Use the infinitive with **to** after these verbs: **want, decide, need, learn, promise, would like / love / hate**:
  I want to go out tonight.
  Jane doesn't need to buy any new clothes.
  Isabelle is learning to play the drums.
  Have you decided to go to the party?

- Use an *-ing* form after these verbs: **like, enjoy, love, hate, finish, go, give up, take up, carry on, throw away, cut down**:
  I don't enjoy cooking.
  I will give up smoking.
  Is Karen taking up judo?

Lesson 33

Subject and non-subject questions in the present simple

Subject question
Who pays Ron? The agency.
(*Who* is the subject of the question.)

Object question
Who does the agency pay? Ron.
(*Who* is the object of the question.)

When a **wh** word is the subject of the sentence, put it before the verb. Don't use an auxiliary verb:
Who supervises Jonathan's work?
NOT ~~Who does Jonathan's work supervise?~~
Who makes the most phone calls? My brother.
What happened? I fell over.

When a **wh** word is the object, use normal question word order, with an auxiliary verb:
Who is Ron talking to? The agency.
What did he say to them? He said . . .

Lesson 34

Relative clauses with *which, that, who* and *where*

- Use **relative clauses** with *who, which, that, where* to define people, places and things:
  A producer is someone who makes TV programmes.
  This is the button which makes it work.
  A kettle is a machine that boils water.
  A garage is a place where you can park a car.

- Use *who* or *that* for people, *which* or *that* for things, and *where* for places.

Lesson 35

Present deduction with *must be, might be, can't be*

- Use **must** + infinitive when you are almost sure something is true:
  I've been travelling for 35 hours. You must be tired.

- Use **can't** + infinitive when you are almost sure something isn't true:
  He can't be thirsty! He's just drunk a litre of water.

- Use **might** + infinitive when you think something is possible:
  I think your car keys might be on the kitchen table.

Lesson 36

Present continuous for future time

- Use the **present continuous** and a time reference (**tomorrow, next week, at ten o'clock**, etc.) to talk about definite future arrangements:
  I'm seeing the doctor at four o'clock.
  They're travelling to Istanbul next Saturday.
  Are we having pasta tonight?

Prepositions of time

- Use **prepositions of time** to say when things happen:

  Use **in** with:
  months, years, the morning, the afternoon, the evening
  She's travelling round Turkey in May.

  Use **on** with:
  days, dates, Christmas day, New Year's day,
  St Valentine's day
  I'm seeing Patrick on Wednesday morning.

  Use **at** with:
  times, Christmas, Easter, breakfast, lunch, dinner
  We're leaving at six o'clock.

> Note: You don't need an article or a preposition with these expressions: *yesterday, tomorrow, this morning / afternoon / evening, last week / month / year, next week / month / year.*
> *I'm seeing Julian next week.* NOT *I'm seeing Julian the next week.*
> OR *I'm seeing Julian in next week.*

Lesson 37

So + adjective / such + noun

- Use **so** + **adjective** to emphasise what you are saying:
  I'm so tired. I can hardly stay awake.
  Tony is so busy at the moment. He has no time at all.

- Use **such** (+ **a / an**) (+ **adjective**) + **noun** to emphasise what you are saying:
  That was such a fantastic night!
  We met such interesting people.
  It was such a surprise!

Lesson 38

Present perfect + for / since

- Use the **present perfect** with **for** and **since** to talk about actions that started in the past and continue now:
  I've lived in the USA for eight months.
  (I live in the USA now.)
  Sam has known Clare since he was twenty.
  (He still knows her now.)
  Peter hasn't had a pet since his dog died five years ago.
  (He still hasn't got a pet now.)
  Has Louise owned that house for a long time?

- Use **for** to talk about the length of time:
  for eight days
  for months
  for a long time

- Use **since** to say when the action started:
  since three o'clock
  since last Tuesday
  since 2000

Lesson 39

Making and responding to suggestions

- Use **let's, why don't we, shall we, what about** and **how about** to make suggestions:

  Let's | sell | the car.   That's a good idea.

  | *Why don't we* *Shall we* | *go* | to the theatre / zoo? | Yes, why not? |

  | *What about* *How about* | *going* | to the sea / cinema? | No, I can't. I'm busy. |

Lesson 40

Second conditional (*if* + past simple + *would / could*)

- Use the **second conditional** to talk about imaginary situations in the present and the future:
  If I had a lot of money, I'd buy a yacht.
  (But I haven't got a lot of money, so I won't.)
  If I became a millionaire, I'd give all my money away.
  (But I probably won't become a millionaire.)

> Note: You can use **were** or **was** with **I, he, she** and **it**:
> *If I were rich . . .   If he were my husband . . .*
> *If it weren't raining . . .   If I was younger . . .*
> *If she was here now . . .*

If + past simple, **would / wouldn't** + infinitive.
OR *If* + past simple, **could / couldn't** + infinitive.

> Note: The *if* clause often comes first but it can come second:
> *If I were richer, I'd be happier.   I'd be happier if I were richer.*
> When the *if* clause comes first, put a comma after it. You don't need a comma when it comes second.

Recording scripts

Lesson 1   A life of achievement

Exercise 6

loved
worked
finished
ended
wanted
moved
acted
used
started

Lesson 2   Billy Elliot

Exercise 6

Billy loves dancing.
He doesn't like running.
What do you like doing?
I really love it.
I quite enjoy it.
I don't like it very much.
I really hate it.

Lesson 3   Hurricane

Exercise 5

P = Presenter in studio
R = Rob, American reporter

P: Now, for the very latest on that hurricane in the USA, we cross live to Rob Kilton in Miami. OK, Rob. What's happening right now? I understand it's bad.
R: Well, we're expecting hurricane Charlie in the next 24 hours. We don't know exactly how big it is but we know it's a big one.
P: What are people doing?
R: Well, lots of people are leaving. Most people don't leave Miami every time there's a weather crisis but this time they are. The roads are full and others are packing up and getting ready to leave.
P: So they're telling people to go.
R: Yes, that's what they're advising, but of course some people stay even during the worst weather conditions.
P: And what are those people doing right now?
R: Most of them are trying to protect their homes. They're covering windows; they're getting food supplies in. Things like that. And of course it's more like London here at the moment. We're all wearing boots and raincoats and hats.
P: But too windy for umbrellas, I imagine.
R: Much too windy.
P: Rob, how often do you get these freak weather conditions?
R: Quite often.
P: So why do people choose to live there?
R: Because it's so beautiful here and the sun always shines ... well, usually.
P: Well, good luck. We're all thinking of you.
R: Thanks. We'll need it.
P: And we'll hear more from Miami later this evening. Now the rest of today's news...

Lesson 4   Possessions we hate

Exercise 2

man
what
car
sofa
day
camera
radio
mini-disk player
watch
laptop
guitar
musical instrument

Exercise 5

P = TV presenter   A = Andrea

P: So please meet tonight's guest. Andrea is here to tell us about things she'd really like to send to Room 101. Hi, Andrea. So what's your first choice?
A: It's my brother Paul's guitar.
P: Your brother's guitar? Why don't you like his guitar?
A: Well he doesn't play it very well and he plays it a lot. It makes a terrible noise.
P: Yes, people who own guitars always think you want to listen to them. I don't like noise so I agree his guitar must go. Send it to Room 101.
A: Thank you.
P: And what is possession number 2?
A: It's this mobile phone.
P: Who does it belong to?
A: It's mine. It rings all the time and I hate that.
P: But you can turn it off.
A: I can't. Sometimes the messages are important. I don't like to turn it off.
P: Exactly. So you need your mobile phone. I'm sorry, you can't put it in Room 101.
A: Oh. OK.
P: And what's the third possession you want to throw away?
A: My TV. Well, it's my parents' TV really.
P: You don't like your TV?
A: That's the problem. I love it. I watch it all the time and I never do any work.
P: Yes, I see what you mean. Are you very busy?
A: Yes, I'm in my last year at university and there's lots of work.
P: OK, then. You have a very good reason, so you can put your TV in Room 101.
A: Thank you ... um, I think.

Lesson 5   A Scottish wedding

Exercise 2

D = Dee   R = Rory

D: Hi, this is Dee Carson and 'Get it Right!'. This week we're talking about Britain and our guest is Rory Graham. Welcome, Rory.
R: Hi.
D: OK, Rory, our first question. Chad Barnes from Kentucky. He wants to know about Scottish weddings.
R: Well, he's asking the right person. I'm Scottish.
D: OK, so ... Chad is going to Scotland this summer and he's going to a Scottish friend's wedding.
R: He'll have a great time!
D: The problem is ... his friend's fiance is from a very traditional family and Chad doesn't know what a traditional Scottish wedding is like. What should he do? What should he wear? And what kind of present should he take?
R: OK. Well, let's start with clothes.
D: He asks: 'Should I wear a kilt?'
R: If you want to, Chad, they'll love it. At an ideal Scottish wedding, all the men wear kilts.
D: Alright, so wear a kilt, Chad! And his next question is: 'What kind of present should I take?
R: It doesn't really matter, but most couples have wedding lists. You should check the list before you buy anything.
D. What about money? Is that a good present?
R: No, not really. You shouldn't give money ... except if the couple ask for it.
D: OK, so a present from the wedding list, not money.
R: Yes, and one other thing ... because you're a friend of the groom, Chad, you should sit on the right hand side of the church.
D: So is that friends of the groom on the right and friends of the bride on the left?
R: Yes. And of course, at the reception, the bride and groom should begin the dancing.
D: So don't dance first, Chad!
R: No, but then dance the night away! Scots really know how to have a good time. Enjoy yourself, Chad.
D: Well, Chad there you have it. I'm really envious. Enjoy!

Lesson 6   Travel with English

Exercise 2

Poland
Italy
Colombia
Australia
Ireland
India
Canada
South Africa

Lesson 7   Why women iron

Exercise 8

1 Girls aren't as fast as boys.
2 Boys are noisier than girls.
3 Women are more talkative than men.
4 Men aren't as tidy as women.
5 Men are messier than women.
6 Schoolboys aren't as hardworking as schoolgirls.
7 Girls aren't as good as boys at football.

Lesson 8 Take a risk

Exercise 2

1 waterskiing
2 scuba diving
3 rock climbing
4 windsurfing
5 snowboarding
6 skateboarding

Exercise 3

D = Dave   A = Andy   P = Paula

D: Hi, everyone. I'm Dave, and welcome to Adventure Zone. Now, let's find out which sports you want to do. OK, and ... you are?
A: Andy Jenkins.
D: Right, Andy. Have you done any dangerous sports before?
A: Yes, I've played football – that's pretty dangerous. And I've been waterskiing and rock climbing, but only once.
D: Waterskiing and rock climbing? When did you do that, then?
A: On my vacation in Greece, last year.
D: And what did you think of them?
A: Well, I really enjoyed waterskiing. But I didn't like rock climbing very much.
D: So, what do you want to try this time?
A: Scuba diving. I haven't done that before. But I've seen it on TV and it looks great. And I haven't been windsurfing. I'd like to try that, too.
D: Right. And you're ...?
P: Paula Benson.
D: Paula Benson ... er, I can't find your name.
P: But I'm not ...
D: Not on the list, I know. Never mind. Have you ever done any of these sports, Paula?
P: Yes, but ...
D: Like what?
P: I've done all of them, lots of times, but ...
D: And you enjoyed them all?
P: Yes, I did, but I'm not here ...
D: OK. But surely there's something you haven't done?
P: No, I've done everything. Look, I'm not here on holiday. I'm the new instructor.
D: Ah ...

Exercise 5

D = Dave   A = Andy

D: Right, Andy. Have you done any dangerous sports before?
A: Yes, I've played football – that's pretty dangerous. And I've been waterskiing and rock climbing, but only once.
D: Waterskiing and rock climbing? When did you do that, then?
A: On my vacation in Greece, last year.
D: And what did you think of them?
A: Well, I really enjoyed waterskiing.

Lesson 9 Job share

Exercise 3

K = Ken   P = Pat

K: Hi. So how were Monday and Tuesday?
P: Busy. Someone wanted one of our male models immediately for a jeans advert. I had to answer the phone every two minutes and hundreds of people left messages. On top of that, Mr Davis was giving me faxes to send, photocopying to do. It was mad.
K: Oh dear ... so what did you do?
P: Not much, I'm afraid. I didn't have time to send these faxes yesterday and I think they're important.
K: Well. Shall I do that for you?
P: Oh, please. And can you phone the photographer? Mr Davis wants to arrange a meeting with him. He asked me to do that yesterday, too.
K: Right. When for?
P: This evening, I think ... yeah, about 8 p.m.
K: This evening? Right. I'll phone him now.
P: Oh, thanks. And he wanted a meeting at Loons Restaurant with the model. Could you phone him too? I forgot. Er, I've got his phone number here somewhere. Ah ... here it is. Oh no, and I didn't book the restaurant! Sorry.
K: Look. I have my own jobs to do for Mr Davis today. I can't do your work too. I'll arrange the meeting with the photographer, but can you make the other calls before you go?
P: Sorry. I can't now. I'm meeting Sally for lunch and I'm already late. Oh – I nearly forgot. Mr Davis wants to see you. He's got a few extra things he needs you to do today.
K: What!

Exercise 6

1 A Can you phone the restaurant, please?
   B Yes, of course.
2 A Could you do this photocopying?
   B Sorry, I'm afraid I can't.
3 A I'll send the faxes today.
   B Thank you.
4 A Shall I arrange a meeting for you?
   B Yes, please.

Lesson 11 Customs change

Exercise 6

They used to throw shoes at the bride.
Poor people didn't use to wear red shoes.

Lesson 12 Win some, lose some

Exercise 3

grapes
bananas
oranges
socks
sandwiches
cigarettes
crisps
toothbrushes
matches
sunglasses
clothes

Exercise 5

Well, this is what happened ...

First, I went to a newsagent's for a newspaper. It cost 50p. I said 'heads' and won. My balance was plus 50p. It felt good!

Then, I went to a café for a coffee. It cost £2. I said 'tails' and won again. My balance was now plus £2.50. Even better!

After that, I went to a clothes shop because I wanted a new t-shirt. It cost £20. I said 'tails' and lost for the first time! I couldn't believe it. My balance went down to minus £37.50.

Next, I went to a convenience store to buy a drink. It cost 53p and I lost again, so my balance went down even more. It was now minus £38.56! Things looked really bad.

I went to a chemist's because I had a terrible headache and I wanted some aspirins! They cost £2.99. I said 'tails' and won! My balance was minus £35.57. It was a bit better.

My headache began to get better too. I went to the hairdresser's to get a new haircut, wash and blow dry. It cost £40. I was really scared. Anyway, I said 'heads' and won! It was great. My balance was plus again ... only plus £4 and 43p, but better than nothing!

In the end, I went to a restaurant to celebrate with a Chinese meal. It cost £15. I said 'tails' and ... won again. My final balance was plus £19.43. Not bad at all. It was really good fun.

Lesson 13 The Ritz

Exercise 1

one thousand five hundred
three hundred
three hundred and thirty-five
two hundred and eighty-five
four million
one thousand and one
eighteen
forty-one
one hundred and fifteen
sixty thousand

Lesson 14 Food for thought

Exercise 2

chocolate
vegetables
onions
bread
cookies
strawberries
lettuce
fruit
oranges
salt
juice
water
yoghurt

Recording scripts

Exercise 6

I have good news today for all you chocolate lovers. Recent studies say chocolate is good for you! But how much chocolate should you eat? Well, a maximum of three chocolate bars a month, so not much. Eating twenty chocolate cookies a day is definitely not a good idea. But remember: chocolate eaters live longer than non-chocolate eaters.

And the same is true for salt. The study from the USA says salt eaters live longer. Now there's a change! Do you have any salt in the house these days?

Another myth from the past is that bread and potatoes make you fat. A new study says, 'Eat a lot of bread and potatoes. You'll lose kilos and get thinner.' Ha! ha! They don't know how many potatoes I can eat.

Do you remember when dentists said, 'Finish meals with fruit?' Well, they now say there is a lot of acid in fruit. It's bad for your teeth so don't eat much fruit.

Finally, they used to say that you shouldn't have any coffee or tea, but now it's OK. Coffee is an anti-depressant: it can make you happy. And ... tea can help you think. So there's food for thought! Happy eating!

Lesson 15 A nice place to work

Exercise 4

I = Interviewer   T = Tom

I: We've come to New York to learn about new office practices in the USA. Tom Banks works for a big law firm here in New York. Tom, do people in your company have to wear smart clothes for work, for example suits?

T: Well, before 1996 we had to wear suits every day. But in 1996 the company introduced dressdown ...

I: Dressdown? What's that?

T: Dressdown means we can wear 'office casual' clothes. We have to wear clothes that look good and we can't wear sneakers or jeans. But we don't have to wear suits and ties and vests any more.

I: This began in 1996?

T: Yeah, but only on Fridays; we didn't have to wear suits on Fridays. Then in 1999 we went to dressdown all the time.

I: Does everyone have to wear 'office casual' now?

T: No, no. You can wear suits if you want to. Some people are happy in suits.

I: And what do you think of the new way of dressing for work?

T: I love it. I'm comfortable in these clothes and suits are expensive so I save money.

I: And do you have to call your boss 'Sir' or 'Miss' or 'Mr' ...?

T: No. We even call the Managing Director by his first name. But, erm, other things? Erm. We don't have to work from 9 to 5, we have flexi-time. For example we can work from 12 to 8, and we don't have to come into the office every day. We can work at home some of the time. The company wants really good people so they make this a really nice place to work.

Lesson 16 Mumbai Soap

Exercise 7

'Mina, you can't leave me,' cries Sanjay, and Mina thinks her heart will break. She thinks about the cricket match in Mumbai where she first met Sanjay. She knows her parents will never accept this man with no money or family connections. And she loves and respects her parents. 'We have found a husband for you,' they say. ' You must get married or go to London and stay with our family there. You'll soon forget Sanjay.'

'Will we see each other again?' asks Sanjay. 'Of course,' promises Mina. 'And I'll write every day.' Her letters tell Sanjay all about her life at the London drama school. But they don't mention Ravi, a family friend in London. 'Marry me, Mina,' Ravi says. Mina asks for time to think. The next day she gets a letter offering her an important role in a popular British soap. When Sanjay hears this, he writes, 'I know you are happy in London. Please forget me.' 'No!' cries Mina.

Five years later, Sanjay turns on the TV in his London hotel room. Tomorrow he will play cricket for India. He knows Mina is in London but he doesn't think he'll see her again. He still remembers her last letter: 'I won't marry anyone else but I must stay in London. It's not just the job ... it's also my family. I'll always love you.' Sanjay can hear her voice. He turns in surprise and sees her on the TV screen. 'She's as beautiful as ever. Is it too late?' he asks himself.

Exercise 9

You'll soon forget him.
She won't marry anyone else.
Will we meet again?
She thinks her heart will break.
I don't think I'll see her again.
Do you think it'll be too late?

Lesson 18 On the move

Exercise 3

K = Katia   M = Mel

K: Hi, Mel. How's it going?

M: Don't ask! I'm in a panic. There's so much to do.

K: When are you going?

M: In a week. This time next week I'll be in Cairo.

K: Wow. You must be excited. Last time we spoke you were trying to sell the car. Have you done that yet?

M: Yes, thank goodness. Someone bought it yesterday so now I can contact the bank and transfer the money. And I've had all my vaccinations.

K: Well done. Did they hurt?

M: Yes – they were horrible, but at least I don't have to worry about them any more. Oh, and my new passport has arrived.

K: Great! What about the visa?

M: No, not yet. They couldn't do that without the passport. But I've talked to someone at the embassy in London. She promised to do it quickly but she hasn't phoned back yet.

K: And what about your ticket?

M: Yes, I've already booked that ... and a hotel room for the first week.

K: So what else have you got to do?

M: Pack the cases ... I haven't done that yet ... but I can't until the last minute really ...

K: When do you start the new job then?

M: The week after next.

K: So it's definite now! You're off!

M: Yes, I hope I'm doing the right thing and that

Lesson 20 The message behind the ad

Exercise 2

1 You'll have shiny hair every time you use Gloss shampoo. So for healthy-looking hair, use it today.

2 Sunease suncream will keep your skin safe from sunburn all through the day. And it keeps your skin soft too!

3 Drink fresh orange juice for breakfast – the healthy way to start your day.

4 Now Lux-Clean washing powder is even better. Your clothes will always be clean and so very soft.

5 This new Tomoto sports car is fast and completely reliable.

Exercise 4

I = Interviewer   A = Advertising Executive

I: Tonight we're talking to Joanna Lindsey, a young and very successful advertising executive. Joanna, when you're making an advert where do you start?

A: Well first, we think about the group of people who might want this product. Are they men or women, young or old, how much money do they have etc.? So, for example, in an ad for an expensive car, we often use young, good-looking men or women who look quite rich. The message is: 'Young, successful people drive this car.'

I: Usually it's the man who drives the car, though, isn't it?

A: Er, yes. That's often true.

I: And he usually has a gorgeous, good-looking girl. So isn't the message really: 'If you buy this car, you'll meet a beautiful woman.' It seems to me that adverts always use sex to sell their products.

A: Not always. For example, with suncream adverts we'd probably use a family. Parents worry about their children so the message here is: 'Your kids won't get sunburnt if you use this suncream.'

I: OK, families for suncream and washing powder, but what about coffee, shampoo?

A: Well, yes, I agree. Sex is used to sell a lot of things from, as you say, coffee to shampoo. Yeah. You'll meet the man of your dreams if your hair is soft and shiny and you drink this delicious coffee. But we also use humour in adverts. People will remember it if it's funny.

I: And ... er, do you like what you do?

A: Yes. It's like making little movies. And, like it or not, adverts sell products. People remember adverts for a long time.

I: Perhaps, but they don't always remember the product – Well, I'm afraid that's all we have time for. Thank you, Joanna Lindsey.

A: Thank you.

Exercise 7

If you buy this car, you'll meet a beautiful woman.
People will remember it if it's funny.
Your kids won't get sunburnt if you use this suncream.
What will happen if I use this shampoo?

Lesson 21 The story of Grace

Exercise 2

Nothing much happened in the sleepy Scottish village of Glentrool. Roddy was standing by the window looking at the rain when Grace ran into the police station. She was crying.

'I've just killed someone. I've just poisoned someone.'

Roddy put the CLOSED sign in the window and locked the door.

'Calm down, Grace, and tell me exactly what happened. Come on, Grace. Tell me. What happened?

Exercise 5

1 Grace was working at home.
2 We were having lunch.
3 They were walking by the river.
4 He was standing near the window.

Lesson 22 Just the job for you

Exercise 7

W = woman, careers officer   M = male student

W: So, what type of job would you like to have?
M: I've been a barman, which is fun. I like working with people. But I'd also like to earn some good money ...
W: And your brother? What job would he like to do?
M: Well, he likes working outside and he loves animals, so he'd like to be a farmer. He'd like to share a farm with me, but I don't know. I like being outside but I wouldn't want to work outside all the time. My perfect job? I'd like to be a pilot. I like travelling and I'd like to visit cities all over the world. I'd really like to learn to fly.

Lesson 23 Made in the USA

Exercise 3

R = Rachel   S = Simon   SH = Stallholder

R: Wow, Simon! This place is fantastic ... so much to buy.
S: Yeah, but be careful. We've only just arrived in San Francisco. And it's not cheap.
R: No, but it's my birthday and I'd love something from Fisherman's Wharf.
S: OK. What do you think of these earrings?
R: Great. Where are they from?
SH: All my silver is bought in Mexico.
R: They're beautiful. How much are they?
SH: 100 dollars.
S: Rachel, that's too expensive.
R: Oh!
S: Come and look at these boxes.
R: Great. What lovely wood. Where are they made?
SH: They're made in Hungary. They're hand-painted.
R: How much are they?
SH: That one's 50 dollars. They're sold for at least 75 dollars in the big stores.
R: It is nice. What do you think, Simon?
S: I think we should look at some other things, then come back later.
SH: Sure!
R: Oh, Simon. Look at these mirrors.
S: I love the colours round the glass.
SH: Everything I sell is made in my family's village in Portugal.
S: That's it, Rachel. I'm going to buy you one of these mirrors.
R: Wait, Simon. I'm not sure I like it best.
S: I do. Look. It's only 10 dollars! Happy Birthday! ... Oh, Rachel?
R: Yes?
S: Could you lend me 5 dollars?

Lesson 24 A long run

Exercise 6

A young couple have an old house.
They turn the house into a small hotel.
You have to go and see the play.
'The Mousetrap' is the longest running play.
He falls in love with an opera singer.
The opera singer loves Raoul.
The Phantom is a young composer.
'Phantom of the Opera' is the most successful musical.

Lesson 26 Australian barbecue

Exercise 3

M = Mike   L = Lisa

M: I've invited Carmen and Julio Gonzalez to a barbie next Saturday.
L: The Argentinians? Good idea.
M: Yeah. It'll be great – a barbie at the beach ... seven of us altogether. I've asked Monica and Jan too ... and your mum. But she's not going to cook. I've promised we'll do everything.
L: Alright. What are we going to cook? Have you decided?
M: Yes, more or less. We're going to start with salads.
L: Good. I can help with that.
M: Good on yeh. What'll you make?
L: Pasta salad ... you know ... my speciality. And then a fruit salad for dessert? I'll need oranges, apples, bananas and pineapple.
M: OK. I'm going to do some shopping tomorrow so I'll buy the fruit and meat then. What shall I get?
L: Oh, the usual. Some beef steak and lamb chops ... and chicken, of course.
M: Oh yeah. Chicken would be great. So, beef steak, lamb chops and chicken.
L: Hey, hang on. Aren't Monica and Jan vegetarians?
M: Oh no! You're right. So we won't have meat ... just vegetables.
L: You gotta be joking. You can't give Argentinians vegetarian food. It's their first Australian beach barbie!
M: No. OK then, I'll make vegetable kebabs for Monica and Jan. We've got plenty of onions, green peppers, tomatoes and mushrooms.
L: Hmmm. Well, I'm glad I eat meat!

Lesson 27 Irritating illnesses

Exercise 2

a headache   D
a sore throat   C
a rash   B
a cold   E
a backache   G
a stomachache   A
an earache   F

Lesson 28 Changing rooms

Exercise 4

P = TV presenter   M = Michelle   J = Jason

P: OK, you can open your eyes now.
M: Oh my goodness. What a change!
J: What have they done?
P: What do you think?
J: Well, it's certainly different.
M: Look at the floor. There's no carpet.
J: And they've polished the floorboards ... oh, I like that.
M: Yes, it's great. The floors are lovely. I'm not sure about the red walls.
J: Hmm, well – it's certainly an interesting colour. I like it ... I think.
M: No, not me. I preferred it how it was.
P: Oh dear.
J   But the curtains look great. They make a real change. They're lovely.
P: Yes, Megan and Peter made those. They're very pleased with them.
J: Yes, and they've moved the sofa. I like it under the window. It's good there.
M: Oh look. Are they new armchairs?
P: No, but they look great, don't they? That was Megan. She hasn't bought new armchairs – just new covers and cushions.
J: Yes, and where's the bookshelf?
P: It's gone, I'm afraid! The first thing they did was remove the bookshelf.
M: I don't mind. I always hated it.
J: But where are the books then?
M: They're up in the cupboard. What a good idea.
P: So all in all, then, what's the verdict?
J: Really nice. Yes, I love it.
M: Me too ... except for those red walls!!

Lesson 29 How rude!

Exercise 3

a Sam, could I use your phone, please?
   Yes, of course.
b Is it OK if I smoke?
   I'm sorry, but it's a no-smoking area.
c Waiter. May I have the bill, please?
   Yes, certainly, Sir.
d Can I give you something towards the meal?
   No. I'll pay. I invited you.

Exercise 5

1 a) May we smoke in here?
   b) May we smoke in here?
2 a) Can I borrow your pen, please?
   b) Can I borrow your pen, please?
3 a) Could I have a glass of water?
   b) Could I have a glass of water?
4 a) Is it OK if I sit here?
   b) Is it OK if I sit here?

Exercise 6

1 May we smoke in here?
   Yes, certainly.
2 Can I borrow your pen, please?
   I'm sorry. I need it myself.
3 Could I have a glass of water?
   Yes, of course.
4 Is it OK if I sit here?
   No, sorry. This seat is taken.

Lesson 30 What would you do for love?

Exercise 5

1 We'd
   We'd live in America.
2 I'd
   I'd buy a boat.
3 They'd
   They'd keep the money.
4 You'd
   You'd love India.
5 He'd
   He'd move to New Zealand.
6 She'd
   She'd stay in England.

Lesson 31 The art of crime

Exercise 5

The Mona Lisa was painted by Leonardo da Vinci, and is probably the world's most famous painting. You can see it in the Louvre, in Paris. But are you sure it was painted by Leonardo da Vinci?

In 1911 the painting was stolen from the museum. Two years later it was offered to an art dealer in Florence by someone called Vincenzo Perugia for 500,000 lire. The art dealer called the police and Perugia was arrested. It seems that the painting was in Perugia's flat for two years. But why?

In fact, the theft was planned by someone called Eduardo de Valfierno. He asked Perugia to steal the Mona Lisa. Then six brilliant copies were made and sold to rich collectors. Each collector thought his copy was the original, and when the painting was found, Valfierno simply told them that it was only a copy. Valfierno was paid for the painting six times, and Perugia was never paid for his help.

So the Mona Lisa was returned to the Louvre. But are we sure that the painting really is the original, and not one of many copies?

Lesson 33 A typical day

Exercise 3

I = Interviewer R = Ron

I: Ron, you have a very unusual job.
R: Yes, I'm a kissogram.
I: And what exactly do you do?
R: Well, I surprise people with a kiss.
I: You kiss people and you get paid?
R: Mmm. That's right.
I: So who employs you?

R: An agency. So if a friend of yours wants to surprise you on your birthday, they can phone the agency. The agency phones me and I come to your party and surprise you ... with a kiss.
I: Who does my friend pay? Does she pay you or the agency?
R: Oh, the agency, and the agency pays me.
I: How long does each job take?
R: The actual job takes about fifteen to twenty minutes, but the preparation takes much longer. My wife, Mary, does that ... she ...
I: Preparation? What preparation?
R: She buys some flowers and a card, and writes a message in the card. When I arrive, I find the birthday girl, give her a kiss and dance with her. Then I get everyone to sing Happy Birthday. I give her the card and read out the message in it, and finally I give the woman the flowers.
I: Doesn't your wife get jealous?
R: No, not really. She drives me to work and drives me home. She always knows where I am. And it's only a job – an unusual job perhaps, but still just a job.

Exercise 8

1 A Who gets up first in your house?
   B Usually I do.
   A And what time do you get up?
   B About 7.30.
2 A Do you have a computer at home?
   B Yes.
   A Who uses it the most?
   B My younger brother.
3 A Who makes the most phone calls?
   B I do, I think.
   A Who do you phone the most?
   B My friend Judith.
4 A Who pays the bills in your house?
   B My mother and father both pay.
5 A Who usually does the cooking?
   B I don't, that's for sure.
   A And who empties the rubbish?
   B Nobody. Look at the mess.
6 A Who do you spend more time with, your friends or your family?
   B My friends.
   A How many evenings a week do you stay at home?
   B Four or five.
   A Who spends the most time in the house?
   B My mother, I suppose.

Lesson 34 How things work

Exercise 2

1 A printer and a photocopier can put pictures or text on paper.
2 A scanner and a digital camera can make pictures that you can look at on a computer.
3 A digital TV has a screen and a remote control.
4 A mobile phone can go in your pocket and rings when someone wants to speak to you.

Exercise 3

screen
keyboard
remote control
computer
printer
laptop
scanner
digital camera
mobile phone
photocopier
digital TV

Lesson 35 What's that noise?

Exercise 4

P = Presenter M = Marion S = Steve

P: You're listening to XS FM on 96 point 3 FM, and it's time for our competition: 'What's the job?' You will hear someone doing his or her job. Guess what the job is and you get four free tickets to a cinema near you. Line one is Marion. Hello, Marion. Are you ready?
M: Yes, Chris. Well, he works somewhere noisy. He might be in a train station or an airport. He might be a bus driver, or a taxi driver. Can I hear a bit more, Chris?
P: OK.
M: Well, he can't be a taxi driver because you pay a taxi driver at the end of the journey. I think I heard a bus. Erm, he must be a bus driver.
P: Yes, he's a bus driver. Marion, you have won four tickets to the cinema. Right, line number two. This is more difficult. Steve.
S: Hi, Chris.
P: Here's your sound, Steve. What's this man's job?
S: Well, he might be a lot of things. He might be an actor in a theatre. He might be a musician at a concert, or a tennis player. Erm. He can't be a football player – it's noisier at a football match.
P: OK. Here's a bit more to help you.
S: Well, he must be some kind of sportsman – that was a body falling. Is he a judo player?
P: Sorry, Steve, and time's up. Here's the full sequence. He's a boxer. So no tickets for Steve. We'll play 'What's the job?' again a little bit later, but right now it's time for the latest weather ...

Exercise 9

1 Next caller. What's this woman's job?
2 Here's a little bit more.
3 And here is your last bit.
4 And here is the full sequence.

Exercise 10

1 And the next caller. Here's your first clue.
2 And here's a little bit more.
3 And here's your last clue.
4 Did you guess it? Well, here's the complete sequence.

Lesson 36 A football fan's website

Exercise 4

C = Charles   P = Peter

C: Hello.
P: Hello. Is that Charles?
C: Yes.
P: Charles, this is Peter Gibson. You know, the guy organising the Manchester United trip.
C: Oh, yes?
P: Just phoning to tell you about a few changes.
C: Not the dates, I hope. I've already asked for time off work.
P: No, no. Nothing as bad as that. Don't worry. It's just that we're leaving on Friday morning at ten o'clock and not twelve o'clock.
C: Fine. So what time are we arriving in Kuala Lumpur?
P: At four o'clock in the morning, Malaysian time, but there'll be a coach waiting at the airport to take us straight to the hotel. We can sleep when we get there.
C: Fine. Anything else?
P: Yes, a couple of things. On Sunday we can't get a coach for the sightseeing tour. We're going to take taxis.
C: Right.
P: And on Monday we're not having dinner at Raffles – it's full. We're going to the Hilton instead.
C: Oh, that's a pity.
P: Yes, sorry about that. And the last thing is nobody wants to go sightseeing on Tuesday so we're going to go shopping instead. I hope that's OK.
C: Yes, that sounds good. I really can't wait. It'll be interesting to see what...

Lesson 37 It was so funny!

Exercise 5

G = Glenda   J = Jim

G: That was such a terrible day. I'm so tired. How about you?
J: Terrible! But I'm feeling generous. Let's go out for once and eat.
G: I'm sorry I was so long.
J: No problem. That's an attractive dress.
G: Thanks.
G: Where are we going?
J: To my favourite restaurant. You'll love it – the food is delicious.
G: I'm so hungry.
J: Me too.
G: Oh Jim, I work with such boring people. And I've been so busy at work.
G: I'm so tired.
J: Me too.
J: We're going to have such a great evening. Let's relax and enjoy it.

Lesson 38 Green card

Exercise 4

I = Investigator   K = Kate

I: So how long have you been in the USA, Miss Bolton?
K: You mean Mrs Bolton. Er. I've been in the USA for eight months but I've only been in New York for five months. I was in Los Angeles before.
I: And how long have you known Mr Bolton?
K: Er... I've known Rod since December, so ... December, January, February March ... Er, I've known him for four months. Yes, we met four months ago.
I: And you've been married for three months?
K: Yes, I saw him at a party and it was love at first sight.
I: Mmmm. I understand. And what do you do, Mrs Bolton?
K: I'm a dancer. I teach dance.
I: Er ... Your neighbour says she has never seen you with your husband.
K: Ah, yes, I can explain that. Er, you see we like very different things. So we don't go out together very often.
I: Ah, I see. OK, Mrs. Bolton. That's all I need to know, thank you. Could I use your bathroom before I go?
K: Bathroom?
I: I think in England you say toilet?
K: Ah, of course. Of course you can.
I: And where is it?
K: Ah, erm, er, yes, where is it? Erm ...
I: Perhaps I do have a few more questions, Mrs Bolton, for you and Mr Bolton.

Exercise 8

I = Investigator   R = Rod

I: Nice cat. Have you had him for a long time?
R: Yes, I've had him for ten years.
I: And how long have you lived in this apartment, Mr Bolton?
R: Since April 15th.
I: And your wife? How long has she been in the USA?
R: Since last September.
I: And how long have you known your wife?
R: For six months.
I: And you've been married since February. Is that right?
R: Yes, we have.
I: And your wife hasn't been to the UK since last September?
R: No, she hasn't.

Lesson 39 Problem solving

Exercise 2

a visit
an invitation
a complaint
a solution
a lie
a suggestion

Exercise 3

J = Jack   B = Becky

J: Look at this mess. We have to tell Dan to leave.
B: Fine. But you invited him to stay with us.
J: Yes, but only for a week. That was two months ago.
B: How about saying your brother's coming?
J: How does that help?
B: We can tell Dan we need the bed.
J: But that's a lie.
B: OK. Shall we tell him the truth? We want him to leave.
J: Mmm. Perhaps the idea about my brother is better.

J=Jane   T=Tom

J: Listen to that! We have to do something. I'm going crazy. Did you talk to Oliver about this?
T: Yes, I did. And he's going to take the dog to training classes.
J: It's so loud.
T: Oh no. Susan's awake again. Ooooohhhh. What about asking him to dinner and we can talk about the problem?
J: Who? The dog?
T: Why don't we buy Oliver a book on dog psychology?
J: Oh, let's just sell the flat! It's the only solution.

Lesson 40 Celebrate

Exercise 6

1 If I had a live band, everyone would dance.
2 I'd have a party on a yacht if money were no problem.
3 If the children didn't come, it wouldn't be such a family occasion.
4 They wouldn't like it if they had to sit down to eat.
5 If you had a party for your friends, where would it be?

Practice section answer key

1 A life of achievement

1 1 a) 2 d) 3 b) 4 c)

2 1 Can you swim?
2 Are you married?
3 How many brothers and sisters have you got?
4 Do you like Madonna?
5 How old are you?
6 Can you play the guitar?
7 Have you got a flat or a house?

3 (1) started (2) didn't have (3) had
(4) wanted (5) didn't want (6) gave
(7) was (8) were (9) worked
(10) decided

2 Billy Elliot

1 1 gymnastics 2 run 3 golf 4 ballet
5 swim

2 1 Jo really hates boxing but he quite likes doing ballet.
2 Ed quite likes playing football and he really enjoys doing ballet.
3 Lou really enjoys playing football and he quite enjoys doing gymnastics.
4 Pam quite enjoys playing football and she really hates boxing.
5 Dave really hates doing ballet but he really loves boxing.

3 1 watching 2 to go / going
3 He usually stays in 4 goes out
5 playing

3 Hurricane

1a) 1 sunhat 2 minus 3 warm 4 degrees
5 scarf

1b) summer

2 1 am wearing – wear
2 Do you usually have
3 isn't wearing
4 is talking
5 doesn't always walk
6 never watches
7 Do you know
8 isn't sleeping

3 1 Do you work in a bank? Yes, I do.
2 Are they doing the shopping?
Yes, they are.
3 Does Carol usually get home before
7 p.m.? No, she doesn't.
4 Is it snowing? No, it's not / it isn't.
5 Are we leaving now? Yes, we are.
6 Do Susan and Francis often visit you on Sunday? No, they don't.
7 Do you know my address? No, I don't.
8 Is Michael having a bath? Yes, he is.

4 Possessions we hate

1 laptop / electric guitar / mobile phone / television / musical instrument / mini-disk player

2 Complete the chart

subject pronoun	possessive adjective	possessive pronoun
I	my	mine
you	your	yours
she	her	hers
he	his	his
we	our	ours
they	their	theirs

3 1 Paul and Jane's 2 Paul and Jane's
3 Jane's 4 Paul and Jane's 5 Paul's
6 Paul's 7 Jane's

4 1 It's their cat. It's theirs.
2 It's their car. It's theirs.
3 It's her mobile. It's hers.
4 It's their hi-fi. It's theirs.
5 They're his magazines. They're his.
6 They're his glasses. They're his.
7 They're her CDs. They're hers.

5 A Scottish wedding

1

groom
guest best man bridesmaid

2 1 Drink lots of water.
2 Don't stay up late at night.
3 Eat lots of vegetables and fruit.
4 Don't drink lots of coffee or tea.
5 Don't sit in front of the computer all day.

3 1 shouldn't read 2 should go 3 should speak 4 shouldn't wear 5 should buy
6 shouldn't be

6 Travel with English

1

2 1 They're / They are going to buy a house.
2 He's / He is going to wash his car.
3 We're / We are going to play tennis.
4 You're / You are going to have a bath.

3 1 d) 2 c) 3 b) 4 a)

7 Why women iron

1 1 talkative 2 aggressive 3 tidy
4 competitive 5 cooperative 6 messy

2 1 competitive 2 messy 3 talkative
4 aggressive 5 tidy 6 cooperative

3 1 happier 2 as talkative as 3 better
4 as tall as 5 correct 6 as bad as
7 thinner 8 faster 9 easier 10 cheap

8 Take a risk

1 1) waterskiing 2) windsurfing
3) rock climbing 4) skateboarding
5) scuba diving

2 1 Has Jack ever visited Scotland?
2 When did Susan first do scuba diving?
3 Have you studied in London before?
4 Has Ken ever lived in Africa?
5 Did we send a card to Dad last week?
6 Did Penny get that bag for her birthday?
7 Did Helen and Lorrie buy their house last year?
8 Have you seen this video before?

3 1 ever 2 haven't 3 have 4 did 5 went
6 good 7 was 8 diving 9 never

9 Job share

1 1 a phone 2 a meeting
3 the photocopying 4 a meeting
5 a report 6 the photocopying

2 1 having / going to have 2 done
3 sent / written 4 arrange 5 write / send
6 send / write 7 answers 8 gets

3 1 I will / I'll meet you at the station tonight.
2 Can you send the information to me, please?
3 Can you pass me the milk, please?
4 Can / Could you carry this for me, please?
5 I'll help you.
6 Can you answer the phone for me, please?
7 Shall I get you a newspaper?
8 Can you open the memo for me, please?

10 Behave yourself

1 1 give / take 2 send / get 3 push / pull
4 borrow / lend 5 remember / forget

2 1 If Jo comes to London, he usually stays
with me.
2 If you smile at people, they often smile
back.
3 She gets angry if we forget her birthday.
4 If they get a letter every week, they are
happy.
5 She goes to the cinema if she has time at
the weekend.

3 1 e) 2 d) 3) c) 4 f) 5 b) 6 a)

11 Customs change

1 1 wore 2 open 3 had 4 wear 5 stay
6 played

2 1 I used to smoke but now I don't smoke
(at all).
2 I used to wear glasses but now I don't.
3 I used to read a lot but now I watch TV.
4 I used to have long hair but now it is short.
5 I used to wear a skirt but now I wear
trousers.
6 I used to cook all the time but now I
never do.
7 I used to ride a bike but now I drive a car.

12 Win some, lose some

1 1 toothbrush 2 matches 3 t-shirt
4 socks 5 sandwiches 6 crisps
7 sunglasses

2 a) socks and t-shirt
b) newspaper and matches
c) sunglasses and toothbrush

3 1 e) 2 d) 3 a) 4 c) 5 f)

4 1 because 2 for 3 because 4 for 5 to

13 The Ritz

1 1 498 2 65,410 3 6,037 4 152
5 5,400,000 6 9,041

2 1 365 2 26 3 28 4 6

3 1 Do / have 2 haven't / have
3 Does / does
4 Has / hasn't / has

4 1 Do you have / Have you got a car?
2 Do they always have coffee after a meal?
3 Does that hotel have many visitors each
month?
4 Do you have / Have you got a headache?
5 Do you have / Have you got any money?
6 Does Tom sometimes have milk in his tea?

14 Food for thought

1 1 strawberries 2 onions 3 vegetables
4 lettuce 5 juice 6 water 7 yogurt
8 cookies

2a) 1 Was there any coffee on the tray?
2 Were there any biscuits … ?
3 Was there any sugar … ?
4 Was there any fruit … ?
5 Were there any sandwiches … ?
6 Were there any cakes … ?
7 Was there any milk … ?
8 Was there any tea … ?

2b) 1 There was some coffee on the tray.
2 There weren't any biscuits … .
3 There was some sugar … .
4 There wasn't any fruit … .
5 There were some sandwiches … .
6 There were some cakes … .
7 There was some milk … .
8 There wasn't any tea … .

3 1 How many t-shirts did you buy?
2 How many photos did you take?
3 How much wine did you drink?
4 How many postcards did you write?
5 How many videos did you watch?
6 How many CDs did you listen to?
7 How much sugar did you put in?
8 How much fruit did you eat?

15 A nice place to work

1 1 pants / trousers 2 vest / waistcoat
3 sneakers / trainers 4 undershirt / vest

2 1 Do you have to work … ? / do
2 Did Thomas have to wear / didn't
3 Does Sara have to wear / do
4 Does Tim have to drive / doesn't
5 Do I have to finish / have to finish
6 has to leave / doesn't have to leave

3 1 He has to work at the weekend.
2 We don't have to call him now.
3 We didn't have to wear a uniform at
school.
4 Did you have to work last Saturday?
5 Jason has to phone his parents when he
gets here.
6 Do I have to have a visa?

16 Mumbai soap

1

love	crime	sport	family
marriage	theft	cricket	husband
passion	prison	football	parents

2 (1) will move (2) won't have (3) will fall
(4) will love (5) will make (6) won't worry
(7) will feel (8) will wake up (9) will speak

3 1 *When* will I start work?
2 *Who* will I meet?
3 *Who* will I fall in love with?
4 *Where* will I get married?
5 *How many* children will I have?
6 *Where* will I live?
7 *How much* will I earn?
8 *Where* will I travel?

17 Camden Market

1 1 attractive 2 popular 3 second-hand
4 unknown 5 trendy

2

adjective	comparative	superlative
quiet	quieter	the quietest
new	newer	the newest
big	bigger	the biggest
busy	busier	the busiest
popular	more popular	the most popular
good	better	the best
bad	worse	the worst

3 1 older than / the oldest / the youngest
2 sadder than / the saddest / the happiest
3 more popular / the most popular / the most
unpopular

18 On the move

1 1 b) 2 d) 3 a) 4 e) 5 c)

2 1 Rent 2 transfer 3 Book 4 pack
5 renew

3 1 Have you rented the car yet?
2 Have you booked the hotel yet?
3 Have you cancelled the newspapers yet?
4 Have you asked the neighbours to feed
the cat yet?
5 Have you bought a new bag yet?
6 Have you packed the case yet?
7 Have you cleaned the house yet?
8 Have you done the food shopping yet?
9 Have you paid the telephone bill yet?
10 Have you phoned for a taxi to the
airport yet?

4 1 I've already rented the car.
2 Sarah hasn't booked the hotel yet.
3 I haven't cancelled the newspapers yet.
4 I haven't asked the neighbours to feed the
cat yet.
5 Sarah has already bought a new bag.
6 I haven't packed the case yet.
7 Sarah hasn't cleaned the house yet.
8 I've already done the food shopping.
9 Sarah has already paid the telephone bill.
10 I haven't phoned for a taxi to the
airport yet.

19 Real fighters

1 1 running 2 skiing 3 cycling 4 dancing
5 boxing 6 training 7 swimming
8 fighting

2 1 skier 2 runs 3 boxes 4 trainer
5 dancer 6 swims 7 cycles 8 fighter

3 1 This artist could draw very well.
2 The young men were quite good at boxing.
3 I couldn't sing very well.
4 Were you good at speaking French?
5 We could ski well when we were young.
6 She wasn't very good at dancing.
7 He couldn't swim very well.
8 They were really good at playing musical
instruments.

20 The message behind the ad

1 1 soft 2 delicious 3 healthy 4 reliable
5 fresh

2 1 If you use this shampoo, your hair will be soft and shiny.
2 If you drink a lot of coffee, you won't sleep.
3 If you try this coffee, you'll love it.
4 If you don't go to bed now, you'll feel tired tomorrow.
5 If you eat more fruit, you won't get ill.
6 If you stop smoking, you'll feel better.
7 If you don't study more, you won't pass your exam.
8 If you buy that coat, you won't have any money to buy the jeans.

3 1 will happen / loses / does / will go
2 is / will you get / is / won't wait
3 loses / will she do / will call / happens
4 asks / will you go / go / will you come

21 The story of Grace

1 1 Peter was talking to Tim when he saw an accident.
2 I was having a bath when you phoned me.
3 We were watching a video when everything suddenly went black.

2 1 was walking 2 saw 3 made 4 was shouting 5 was crying 6 didn't stop
7 ran 8 started 9 heard 10 realised
11 were acting 12 were making

3 1 What was the man doing when Helen saw him?
2 What was the woman doing?
3 Why did Helen laugh?
4 What were the people doing?

22 Just the job for you

1 1 is creative
2 works alone
3 works with animals
4 doesn't travel very often
5 works with animals

2 1 Does / does / Would / would
2 Would / don't
3 Would / wouldn't / Do / do / would
4 Do / does / doesn't / would

3 1 Would Tom like to be a pilot?
2 Does Helen like working with children?
3 Do Sam and Fran like acting?
4 Would you like to do a more creative job?
5 Do you like working with Harry?

23 Made in the USA

1 4 metal tray 1 leather jacket 7 cotton socks
5 glass ashtray 6 gold pen 3 silver fork

2 1 Nissan cars are made in Japan.
2 Stamps are sold in a post office.
3 Where is this Scandinavian furniture sold?
4 Are Spanish oranges sold in British supermarkets?
5 These earrings aren't made out of gold.
6 Brazilian coffee is sold all over the world.
7 Leather jackets are made in Turkey.
8 Is a lot of chocolate bought in Belgium?

3 1 sell 2 is bought 3 is made 4 buy
5 don't sell 6 is bought 7 make
8 is bought and sold

24 A long run

1

2 1 the 2 seats 3 the 4 stage 5 the
6 actors 7 chairs 8 a 9 game 10 The
11 the 12 singer 13 The 14 audience

3 1 an / a / the / the
2 A: a
B: a / a
3 a / The / the / the
4 a / the / a / the / a / the

25 Smart agreements

1 1 forget 2 make 3 lose 4 make

2 1 When do we have to leave the party?
2 How much did you have to pay for a taxi?
3 What do you have to do at work tomorrow?
4 Why does Pat have to visit his grandparents?
5 How long do you have to wait for the bus?
6 What time do I have to phone you this evening?

3 1 You mustn't talk / speak.
2 You mustn't fish.
3 You mustn't park.
4 You mustn't cycle.
5 You mustn't stop.
6 You mustn't enter / go in.

4 1 mustn't 2 mustn't 3 don't have to
4 doesn't have to 5 doesn't have to
6 don't have to 7 mustn't

26 Australian barbecue

1
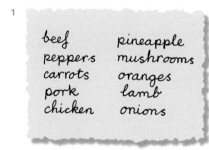

beef   pineapple
peppers   mushrooms
carrots   oranges
pork   lamb
chicken   onions

2 1 A: are you going to B: (I)'ll A: (I)'ll
2 A: are going to B: (I)'ll
A: aren't going to / (We)'re going to
3 A: are you going to
B: (Pete)'s going to B: (I)'ll

27 Irritating illnesses

1 stomach chin nose eye ear arm
mouth throat tooth head

2 1 backache 2 rash 3 headache 4 cold
5 stomachache 6 earache 7 sore throat

3 1 boring 2 frightened 3 worrying
4 surprised 5 interesting 6 depressed
7 shocked 8 embarrassing

4 1 boring 2 shocking 3 surprised
4 frightening 5 depressed 6 interesting

28 Changing rooms

1

2 1 The runner has won a race.
2 Charlie has had an accident.
3 The woman has not gone out.
4 They have seen a film.
5 The child has broken a plate.
6 The couple have painted the room.
7 Grandpa has gone to sleep.
8 The cat hasn't finished its food.

29 How rude!

1 1 He's kissing a girl.
2 He's got his elbows on the table.
3 He's eating with his fingers.
4 He's pointing at a waiter.
5 He's blowing his nose.

2 2 c) 3 d) 4 b) 5 a) 6 e)

3 1 Can I leave ... 2 Sorry. I'm ...
3 Is it okay if ... 4 No, I'm sorry ...

30 What would you do for love?

1 1 go 2 stay 3 find 4 agree (to do something) 5 tell the truth 6 sell
7 get married

2 1 borrow 2 sell 3 agreed 4 Tell
5 refused 6 moved 7 lies 8 lost

3 1 I'd buy that jacket.
2 Would you lend a stranger some money?
3 I wouldn't lie to my friends.
4 They wouldn't move to Prague.
5 Would you spend that much money on a car?
6 Janet would tell me the truth.

31 The art of crime

1 1 robbery / robbers / robbed 2 burglary / burglars 3 murder / murdered / murderer

2 1 enjoyed 2 took 3 left 4 was stolen
5 were woken 6 were taken 7 bought
8 was taken

3 1 were given / found 2 were told / started
3 made / were asked 4 was asked / lost
5 was cancelled / were given 6 was given /
didn't like

32 Willpower

1 1 Cut down on sugar. 2 Throw away old
clothes. 3 Take up Tai Chi classes. 4 Carry
on doing exercises every morning.

2 1 Mary and John gave up smoking three
years ago.
2 I want to cut down on the number of
calories I eat.
3 Are you going to carry on learning Spanish
after the holiday?
4 Lucy wants to give up eating chocolate but
she can't.
5 We should carry on phoning her even if
she doesn't answer.

3 1 to see 2 to visit 3 waiting 4 to phone
5 smoking 6 dancing

33 A typical day

1 1 employ 2 paid 3 make 4 do
5 empty

2a) Jack

2b) 1 When does Jack get up?
2 Who is never late for class?
3 Who catches the 8.40 a.m. bus?
4 Who gets up at 6 a.m.?
5 Why does Jack get angry?
6 Who spends hours in the bathroom?
7 When does Jane leave the house?

34 How things work

1 1 a photocopier 2 a digital TV / television
3 a scanner 4 a printer 5 a mobile phone
6 a digital camera

2 1 mobile phone 2 scanner
3 photocopier 4 digital camera 5 printer
6 digital TV / television

3 1 which / that   digital TV / television
2 who   photographer
3 where   airport
4 which / that   cooker
5 who / that   chef
6 which / that   dictionary
7 which / that   scarf
8 which / that   digital camera

35 What's that noise?

1 1 cheered 2 screamed 3 yawned
4 cried

2 1 She must be Australian.
2 He might be asleep.
3 He can't be American.
4 Jack must be rich
5 Ben might be ill.

3 3 a) 4 b) 5 b) 6 a) 7 b) 8 a)

36 A football fan's website

1 1 a) x b) on 2 a) in b) x 3 a) x b) at
4 a) in b) x 5 a) in b) x

2 1 ~~in~~ on 2 ~~on~~ at 3 ~~at~~ in 4 ~~in~~ x 5 at
6 ~~on~~ in 7 on 8 ~~at~~ x

3 1 Is Ken coming to the party next Friday
evening?
2 I'm not going to my Japanese lesson
tonight.
3 Are we having spaghetti for supper this
evening?
4 What are you doing on Thursday evening?
5 Sue and Dan aren't going skiing in January.
6 Is Betty having her driving test on Tuesday
morning?
7 Ken and Mary are having lunch at 1 p.m.
8 I am meeting Jo and Fred on Saturday
evening.

> Note: 4, 6 8: no preposition needed in US English.

37 It was so funny!

1
great	terrible
generous	mean
special	ordinary
attractive	ugly
funny	serious
delicious	horrible
full	hungry

2 1 terrible / horrible 2 great / attractive
3 terrible / hungry

3 1 so 2 such 3 so 4 such 5 so
6 such

4 1 It was such a good cake.
2 He was such a tall man.
3 It was such a surprise.
4 The wind was so strong.
5 It was such a long story.
6 Your house is so lovely.

38 Green card

1 1 permit 2 visa 3 card 4 licence

2 1 card 2 licence 3 card 4 visa
5 immigration 6 permit

3 1 I've known Matt since 1980.
2 I haven't had this job for long.
3 Sally hasn't been to London since 1999.
4 Have you seen John since his birthday?
5 How long have you had your driving
licence?
6 We haven't eaten any chocolate for ages.
7 They haven't visited Frank since June.

4 1 Julian's worked at Ford for two months.
2 Susan's had her leather jacket for four
years.
3 We've lived in this house since July.
4 Peggy's known David since 2000.
5 Lucy's had her car since her birthday.
6 I've been a teacher since 1995.
7 Lorna and Ian have been divorced for a
few months.

39 Problem solving

1
noun	verb
solution	solve
invitation	invite
visit	visit
suggestion	suggest
lie	lie
complaint	complain

2 1 complain 2 suggestion 3 invitation
4 lie 5 visit 6 complaints 7 invited

3 1 about coming 2 send 3 don't you buy
4 about phoning 5 invite 6 don't we
complain

4 1 watching 2 Let's stay 3 It's 4 Why
don't we 5 How about selling 6 Shall we
buy Sam 7 I'm too 8 go

40 Celebrate

1

2 1 If I knew her e-mail address, I'd tell you.
2 If she had enough money, she'd eat out
tonight.
3 If Kim studied hard, she'd pass her exam.
4 If I did some sport, I'd be fit.
5 If I didn't feel tired, I'd play football today.
6 If I had my credit card with me, I'd buy
that jacket.
7 If I had time, I'd help you.
8 If I knew his address, I'd invite him to the
party.

Pearson Education Limited

Edinburgh Gate, Harlow
Essex CM20 2JE, England
and Associated Companies throughout the world

www.language-to-go.com

Language to go is a trademark of Pearson Education Limited

© Pearson Education Limited 2002

First published 2002
Seventh impression 2007

Set in 10/13pt Neue Helvetica Medium and 10/13pt Univers Light

Printed in China CTPSC/07

ISBN 13: 978-0-582-403-97-0

Author acknowledgements

We would especially like to thank the following people: Amybeth and Emma for their continued support; all those colleagues and students, especially at International House and Bell language schools, who have helped us develop our ideas over the years; Bernie Hayden (Project Manager); Judith King (Publishing Manager); Simon Greenall (Series Editor); Suzanna Harsányi (Editorial Director) and Frances Woodward (Senior Publisher); Beth Sims and Fiona Beddall (Editors); Sally Lace (Designer); the rest of the Longman team.

Publishing acknowledgements

The publishers would like to extend thanks to the freelance editorial team. We are indebted to Bernie Hayden, Senior Development Editor for the whole series and Project Manager of the Elementary and Pre-Intermediate levels, for his outstanding contribution to *Language to go*. Special thanks are due to Fiona Beddall and Beth Sims for all their excellent work as editors. We would also like to acknowledge with thanks Kenna Bourke for her writing of the Grammar reference.

The publishers and authors are very grateful to the following people and institutions for reporting on the manuscript:
Andrzej Antoszek, College of English/The Catholic University of Lublin, Poland; Patrycja Baran, College of English/The Catholic University of Lublin, Poland; Mariusz Mirecki, Lingua Nova, Lublin, Poland; Adam Kunysz, The Catholic University of Lublin/A1 School of Foreign Languages, Poland; Anne Vernon James, IFG Langues, Paris; Philippa Dralet, Le Comptoir des Langues, Paris; Celso Frada, Evoluta Idiomas, São Paulo; Sarah Bailey, Lexis Instituto del Idioma, Málaga; Helen Hadkins, British Language Centre, Madrid; Stephanie Oliver, International House, Milan; James Tierney, The British Council, Milan; Wendy Abu-Saad, The New School of English, Cambridge; Christopher Reakirt, The New School of English, Cambridge; Steve Baxter, UK; Phyllis Vannuffel, ITS Hastings; Rolf Donald, Eastbourne School of English; Jennie Kober, Anglo English School, Hamburg; Nicholas Miller, Elvis Language School, Prague, Czech Republic; Jodi Bennett, The Language House, Prague, Czech Republic; David Todd, ILC Prague, Czech Republic; Shaun Wilden, Akcent, IH Prague; Maria Eugenia Batista, Brazil. We would also like to thank Robert Mass for his contribution to Lesson 15.

Designed by Sally Lace

Series design by Steve Pitcher

Cover design by Juice Creative

Back cover photographs of the authors by Trevor Clifford

Illustrated by: Andrew Baker, Clinton Banbury, Kathy Baxendale, Stanley Chow, Linda Clark, Ian Dicks, Sophie Grillet, Paul Hampson, Dave Hayden, Tony Husband, Alison Lang, Maltings Partnership, Gillian Martin, Louise Morgan, Pierre-Paul Pariseau, Gavin Reece

Picture research by Hilary Fletcher

We are grateful to the following for their permission to reproduce copyright material and photographs:
©Abode for page 58 (top), 59 (right); ActionPlus/Steve Bardens for page 18 (d), /Slide File for page 19 (top), /Neale Haynes for page 43 (top right); All Action/Harry Siskind for page 5 (top); Allsport/Dave Rogers for page 16 (bottom), /©Hulton Deutsch for page 25 (bottom left); Aquarius Library for page 5 (bottom); Associated Press, AP/Chris Pizzello, Stringer for page 53 (left), /Simon Thong, Stringer for page 74 (bottom); The Bridgeman Art Library/Louvre, Paris, France; Britstock-IFA/ICS/Fabricius & Taylor for page 9, /West Stock Fotopic for page 46 (bottom right); Camera Press, London/(RING/RBO) London for page 41 (left); ©Chika, all rights reserved for page 40; Collections/John D Beldom for page 36 (right); Corbis Stock Market/Paul Barton for page 78 (top), /Jon Feingersh for page 39, /Bob Krist for page 46 (top right), /Larry Williams for page 78 (bottom); ©Daily Mail for pages 26 (middle), 27 (left, right, middle left); The Edinburgh Photographic Library/Alex Gillespie for page 12; EPS/Derek Santini for page 41 (right); Mary Evans Picture Library for page 25 (bottom right); Hulton Deutsch for page 25 (top left): The Image Bank/Daniel E.Arsenault Photgraphy Inc. for page 73 (e), /Barros & Barros for page 20 (right), /Britt J.Erlanson-Messens for page 16 (top), /Ghislain & Marie David de Lossy for page 20 (left), /Donata Pizzi for page 73 (b), /Sparky for page 46 (bottom left); ImageState/AGE Fotostock for page 52; Impact/Martin Black for page 26 (left); ©IPC for page 58 (bottom); Katz Pictures/©Emma Boam 2000D for page 90; Mirisch-7 Arts/United Artists (Courtesy Kobal) for page 51 (bottom); PA Photos for page 53 (right); The Photographers Library for page 46 (middle left); Pictor International for pages 14 (bottom), 43 (left), 72 (a); Pictorial Press for pages 50, 51 (top), /©2000 Universal for page 6; Popperfoto/Simon Bruty for page 18 (f); Powerstock Zefa for pages 36 (left), 48, 72 (f), 73 (c), /Benelux Press for page 43 (bottom right), /Index Stock Photography for page 18 (c); Rex Features for page 26 (right), /SIPA for page 4; ©Ritz, London for pages 28, 29; ©Sony for page 35 (TV); Stone/Lori Adamski Peek for page 14 (top), /David Ball for page 15 (bottom), /John Beatty for page 46 (top left), /Christopher Bissell for page 73 (d), /Stewart Cohen for pages 15 (top), 21 (top), /Ben Edwards for page 57, /G.D.T for page 73 (h), /Zigy Kaluzny for page 32, /Kaluzny/Thatcher for page 21 (bottom), /David Madison for page 18 (e), /Jake Rais for page 78 (background); ©Superstock for page 82; Telegraph Colour Library/Ian D.Cartwight (AVALON) for page 72 (g), /NONO for page 27 (middle right), /Philippe Gelot for page 30 (bottom), /Richard Price for page 18 (a), V.C.L for page 46 (bottom middle); Topham Picturepoint for page 25 (top right); World Pictures for page 48 (left).

The following photographs were taken on commission for Pearson Education by:
Trevor Clifford for pages 25 (frames), 30 (top), 31, 34, 35, 48 (objects), 54, 59 (left), 74 (top).

Front cover photographs left to right:
Photo Disc; Powerstock Zefa; Superstock; Superstock; Corbis Stock Market.